Negotiation
Basics

Negotiation
Basics

**Concepts,
Skills,
and Exercises**

Ralph A. Johnson

SAGE Publications
International Educational and Professional Publisher
Newbury Park   London   New Delhi

For information address:

SAGE Publications, Inc.
2455 Teller Road
Newbury Park, California 91320
E-mail: order@sagepub.com

SAGE Publications Ltd.
6 Bonhill Street
London EC2A 4PU
United Kingdom

SAGE Publications India Pvt. Ltd.
M-32 Market
Greater Kailash I
New Delhi 110 048 India

Printed in the United States of America

Library of Congress Cataloging-in-Publication Data

Johnson, Ralph A.
  Negotiation basics: concepts, skills, and exercises / Ralph A.
Johnson.
    p.   cm.
  Includes bibliographical references and index.
  ISBN 0-8039-4051-3 (cl).—ISBN 0-8039-4052-1 (pb)
  1. Negotiation. I. Title.
BF637.N4J64 1993
158'.5—dc20   92-35503
                                                                    CIP

96 97 98 99 00 01 10 9 8 7 6 5 4 3

Sage Production Editor: Tara S. Mead

Contents

Acknowledgments

My colleagues Judi Catlett, Ed Brown, Jill Kriesky, and Hig Roberts have shared their experiences, ideas, and observations on negotiation practices throughout the years. Tara Mead and Harry Briggs, editors at Sage, provided help and guidance with this project. John Gever read the manuscript and offered valuable suggestions. Vicki Johnson contributed counsel and support from the beginning. I am deeply grateful to each of them.

Introduction

Until recently, everyday conflicts were settled by traditional authority or custom. Fathers spoke for the family; kings made laws for the nation; bosses ruled the workplace; and teachers made decisions in the classroom. Society's decision makers had power and respect through their roles, but they also had responsibility for their decisions. They lived with the uneasiness of knowing that the subjects might rebel at any time. Subordinates, on the other hand, were told what to do and were expected to obey. Their choices were restricted, but they were exempt from worry about weighty decisions. Local custom provided answers to everyday disputes; tradition designated the specific person who handled any unprecedented problems. The established practice imposed tight limits on the role of both superior and subordinate. What it offered was the security of clear rules.

As long as the world changed slowly, people were inclined to revere the past as the treasure chest of answers. The dramatic changes throughout the last half of the twentieth century undermined traditional life and created a demand for new ways of productive human interaction in a volatile world. New conditions have given rise to a new interest in negotiation. In Washington, DC, the U.S. Department of Labor promotes a "new" approach to labor-management negotiations for experienced bargainers (Barrett, 1990). Across the continent, children in Los Angeles learn negotiation methods in elementary school (Gordon, 1990).

If changing technology and expanded travel opportunities offer new prospects, new perspectives, and new ways of living, they also raise new doubts about the value of tradition (Mankin, 1977). Exploding populations, urban population concentrations, multinational corporations, worldwide communication networks, and a global economy work to render conventional wisdom obsolete. The deterioration of the earth's resources, the number of politically oppressed peoples, spectacular technological advancements, and greater social, economic, and technical interdependence produce new conflicts as they increase the demand for human interaction. With tradition now an unreliable guide, a weak enforcer, or simply an irrelevant force in multicultural situations, humans are forced to continue the search for new methods of dealing with each other. What are the standards of fairness? What are reasonable expectations? How are people supposed to relate to each other? In many cases, the answers to these questions are negotiated. In commercial transactions, government regulation or the market has generally dominated many of the economic decisions. Government regulations are often the result of multiparty negotiation.

In the private sector, supply and demand may control parameters of costs and prices, but both can be influenced by human intervention. Demand can be manipulated by aggressive advertising and sales campaigns, and supply can be controlled by monopolistic corporations. Because supply and demand often stem from human decisions rather than some inevitable force, negotiations play a role in shaping those market forces.

In legal disputes, the pursuit of court-imposed remedies burden and backlog the judicial systems, making alternative dispute resolution methods more attractive (Alward, 1984). Government agencies and corporations increasingly seek negotiated rather than litigated resolutions to disputes (Dunlop, 1984). As the twenty-first century approaches, there are new opportunities and obligations to negotiate.

Negotiated relationships are sometimes called "positive-sum games," desirable because they add to human welfare. They are positive in the sense that each side is a responsible party acting in an enlightened way with an understanding that other parties have a right to pursue enlightened self-interest, that shared decisions produce better end results for both parties, and that negotiating often serves as an alternative to the high costs of preparation, production, and maintenance of force. People deliver their best efforts if they understand and agree to the terms of their lives. Negotiation allows all sides that opportunity.

Great artists and athletes often make their work look effortless, as if they never had to practice, as if they were born to sing, to run. Talented cooks move around the kitchen with spontaneity, seeming to have no method, no direction; a dash of this, a pinch of salt, and, presto, here is a masterpiece! Skilled negotiators exude that easy, almost careless confidence; a proposal, maybe a couple of counterproposals, and like magic it looks like a great agreement!

Certainly, for a very few, natural talent or a single-minded dedication produces their exceptional performance in a million-dollar deal, but that picture is misleading. Negotiation skills come from work and application of sound principles. Because individual happiness and success depend on a personal ability to reach positive agreements and to reject or alter less than desirable deals, negotiation is an essential part of everyday life. It is not just a profession for a few.

What does it take to become a skilled negotiator? Aspiring negotiators might look for models of success and imitate their style. By reading exciting accounts of high stakes and big deals, they hope to learn the secrets. Unfortunately, as they try to apply some of the techniques, they experience failure because they lack the spectacular talent or the driving desire to commit their lives to a solitary endeavor.

Another alternative is to follow a prepackaged plan for each particular negotiating problem in the hopes of achieving success. There are a variety of ready-made models outlining steps for buying a car, selling a house, or pressuring the boss for a salary increase (Weiss-Wik, 1983). But contemporary life requires the ability to adapt to many types of transactions every day. Recipes fail to prepare their practitioners for the unknown or unfamiliar.

This book offers another method. In an effort to help students learn and experience negotiations from both a theoretical and a practical perspective, each chapter explores and discusses a major negotiating concept; the concept is then linked to a related skill necessary for negotiating success. Broad guidelines for applying the skills and concepts are integrated into the text. Finally, exercises drawn from everyday negotiating problems are furnished to simulate the experiences related to the topic.

The merger of concepts, skills, and exercises is designed to make classroom learning relevant and worthwhile and to provide a basis for continued skill acquisition. For teachers and students, it is easier to examine and understand topics if they are connected to a concrete problem. The exercises offer a chance to experiment without the encumbrance of the real-world costs of trial and error.

Everyday transactions between individuals are different than formal collective negotiations among large organizations, but the topics and guidelines apply to all types of negotiation. Except for the eighth chapter, each discussion applies to both individual and collective negotiations.

The overall purposes of this book are

1. to demonstrate how negotiation works,
2. to outline options and procedure for negotiation preparation,
3. to identify the common negotiating problems and deficiencies, and
4. to show how skill building can be integrated into preparation for negotiation.

The first chapter, "Transforming Problems into Negotiating Opportunities," defines negotiation and examines the criteria for recognizing a negotiating opportunity. Knowledge of what constitutes a negotiating opportunity eliminates the problems and frustrations of being fooled, but it also helps identify those situations with an opportunity for mutual profit. Perceptual orientations are discussed here because negotiators who are willing to assess and modify their patterns of viewing the world may have an advantage in recognizing opportunities for negotiation.

Chapter 2, "Identifying and Pursuing Useful Negotiating Goals," outlines the steps necessary for building goals. Without a precise picture of what they want and a plan to achieve it, negotiators head toward disaster or at least dissatisfaction. Because successful goals are often a result of the negotiator's ability to hear and understand the issues on both sides, steps for building "active" listening skills are included.

Most talks occur without the participants possessing complete, relevant information. The third chapter, "Finding and Using Information," reviews the role of information in negotiations. What kinds of information does a negotiator need? Where can it be found? How should it be used? Because those who are skillful at eliciting valuable information have an important strategic edge, this chapter examines techniques for asking productive questions.

To be effective at the process of give-and-take, a negotiator must be able to calculate the costs associated with each proposal. Chapter 4, "Making Cost-Benefit Decisions," analyzes "costs," including many of the hidden and incidental costs. Here the steps necessary for making an accurate and comprehensive cost-benefit analysis are outlined.

Power is obvious in many negotiations but present and relevant in all of them. The fifth chapter, "Building Credibility to Enhance Your Power," analyzes bargaining power by categorizing the methods available for inducing others to comply with proposals. The discussion explores the sources and roles of bargaining power in negotiation situations. The chapter presents ways that a negotiator can build the personal credibility that is necessary for applying or resisting power negotiating.

Individuals lose much of their negotiating potential if they adopt one approach and use it for every situation. They also lose advantages if they fail to identify the other side's strategy. Historically, people have tried to reach favorable agreements by ingratiation, by intimidation, by reciprocity, and by applying principles that would provide them with higher odds of success. Chapter 6, "Fitting Strategies to Your Situation and Personal Style," examines these four popular approaches or "strategies." Each is presented along with its advantages, disadvantages, and optimum application. Here, there is a discussion of the ways negotiators can explore and understand their own personalities as they select and implement appropriate strategies.

Even after thorough preparations, negotiators should be ready to make adaptations once the talks begin. The seventh chapter, "Choosing the Appropriate Tactics," examines "table tactics" that a negotiator may encounter or use. Because negotiators who are prepared for diversionary tactics are better equipped to stay on course in pursuit of their own goals, this chapter suggests ways to manage distractions.

Chapter 8, "Organizing Constituents for Representative Bargaining," explores the role of an agent who speaks on behalf of someone else. It summarizes the relationship between constituents and those who speak on their behalf. It includes criteria to use in selecting a spokesperson. Representative negotiation requires mutual support and communication between the representative and the represented. The discussion explores the potential for an active and useful constituent role. It provides perspectives for examining constituent concerns as well as ways of unifying and mobilizing them.

The ninth chapter, "Searching for Secrets to Break Impasses," suggests reasons that talks fail and proposes appropriate measures that negotiators may employ for breaking impasses. The

criteria for analyzing nonverbal messages are presented here as a
guide for negotiators to detect movement on the other side and
discern when impasses are developing and dissolving.

When parties are unable to reach an agreement on their own,
they may need to turn to "third-party intervention" to bring about
a settlement. Chapter 10, "Using an Outside Party When You Need
One," gives a negotiator's perspective in the suggestions for selecting and using outsiders to help reach a settlement.

Negotiators can often avoid third parties and achieve success
on their own if they are able to build a positive climate. The final
chapter, "Conclusion: Creating a Positive Negotiating Climate,"
presents some ways that the negotiator can build the desired
emotional climate.

Knowledge, experience, skill, common sense, and desire determine how successfully you can turn the suggestions here into
great results. You can teach yourself to improve and build your
competencies, but achieving consistent success in the variety of
negotiating situations that you are likely to encounter demands

1. understanding the negotiation process,
2. commitment to improving the necessary skills, and
3. work, preparation, study, and continuous reevaluation.

For some, learning the basic concepts may be easy, while others
will have an easy time building skills. As experience grows, some
make the process look easy and others appear methodical and
mechanical. The amount of effort applied to preparation is one
crucial difference between negotiators. Poor work may be the
greatest vulnerability in negotiators, but often it is also the major
factor that an individual negotiator can control. Sloppy preparation, boredom, fatigue, a search for shortcuts, impatience, or competing activities diminish the chances of success.

The skilled negotiator is not just one who has the strength to
achieve victory or hold firm against a powerful adversary but one
who also has the wisdom to know when cooperation is possible
and mutually beneficial. When two people or two sides have the
ability and willingness to take a risk in pursuit of a larger purpose,
they may have discovered the best that negotiation has to offer.
Learning about negotiation enhances your chances of successful

transactions, but it also increases the likelihood of better settlements and more reasonable proposals for others (DeNisi & Dworkin, 1981). The hope is not only for you to be more successful but for the negotiation process to be more successful as a method of helping all of us, with all of our differences, to live and work together productively.

Transforming Problems
Into Negotiating Opportunities

The Story of the Impossible Roommate

Tim and Abdul are seniors at a large midwestern university. Both spent the first 3 years living in a dorm, where the two became acquainted. At the end of last semester, after successfully completing a class project together, Tim said he could secure a great deal on an attractive, convenient apartment. He proposed that if the two of them shared expenses they could live almost as cheaply in an apartment as they could on campus.

Abdul agreed and found that he loves the apartment and being away from dorm life, but he is not happy having Tim as a roommate. It seems to him that Tim makes all the rules but accepts none of the responsibilities. For example, Tim has strong, definite tastes in furnishings and expects Abdul to kick in half the money for items that Abdul dislikes. Tim dismisses Abdul's choices as either being out of sync with the apartment or lacking in quality. Abdul believes that there is not much give-and-take in the relationship. Tim ridicules Abdul's taste in music and sometimes even turns it down or off without asking. Tim is a personal slob and does not contribute to cleaning the place. He often invites friends over without giving Abdul any notice. Generally, Abdul feels that Tim doesn't want to reach a joint agreement, he just wants to do whatever pleases him at the moment. Because Abdul has never been one for confrontation, he has let a lot of the small irritations pass, but, when he tries to discuss the situation, Tim either belittles the problem or says that Abdul is making a major issue out of small misunderstandings.

1

At this point, Abdul thinks he has made a mistake by allowing Tim to make all of the financial arrangements on the apartment. Tim has the lease in his own name, but Abdul has contributed half the deposit and half of the rent. He already has made a substantial financial investment and does not feel that he could leave at this point. He made a commitment to the arrangement and technically Tim has paid his share. Also, he could never find similar living quarters for this low rent. And, during the school year, little is available. To add to his stress, his grades have fallen and he is lagging behind in every class. He knows that he does not have time to search for new accommodations.

Abdul can improve his situation by negotiating with Tim. His first step should be to identify what it would take to transform this troubled relationship into an opportunity for negotiation.

Negotiation is a process in which individuals or groups seek to reach goals by making agreements with others. This process often includes offering concessions and demanding them from other parties, but it functions best when it serves as a method for discovering mutual interests and joint payoffs.

People are motivated to act when they feel aggrieved, worried, or insecure, or when they need a change. The urge to negotiate comes when they find that what they want or need is available only at the cost or in the form they desire through someone else. Otherwise, they could get what they want on their own. Negotiation is not passive. It is a commitment and a procedure that requires dealing with others actively. It is a struggle for a solution.

Negotiation takes many forms:

- It may include many people or only two.
- It may focus on one simple problem or many complex issues.
- It may be concluded in one session or may be an ongoing process.
- It may be a formal ritual or an informal conversation.
- It may be an effort to maintain a relationship or endorse changes.

Despite these differences, all negotiations share some common features. For negotiation to occur, the following conditions must be present:

- At least two parties must be involved. Individual people, factions, organizations, or nations could qualify as a "party" in negotiation.
- Each party needs a sense of its own interest and purpose; it aims to accomplish something for its side through the assistance or compliance of another party.
- Each party must understand the role and needs of the other party and be willing to exchange and examine proposals in an attempt to reach agreement.
- Each party must be convinced that negotiations will offer it some relief, opportunity, or profit.

Identifying Negotiation Opportunities

The ability to identify a potential negotiating opportunity is a powerful, useful skill; the ability to discern who and what to avoid may be even more useful. In many situations, negotiators may have some choice as to who their negotiation counterpart will be. Sondak and Bazerman (1989) found that recognizing and "matching" with those who are willing and able to negotiate productively is an important skill. Not only do poor matches waste time and resources, but a bad agreement may be worse than no agreement.

The word *negotiation* suffers from overuse. It commonly refers to almost any kind of interaction between individuals or groups. Negotiation looks like many other activities, so it is an easy activity to fake. Strong parties may want the kind of efficiency and control that unilateral decision making offers. If they also want to create the feelings of partnership and shared responsibility that negotiations offer, they may engage in processes that look much like genuine negotiations, even as they seek to avoid or undermine genuine negotiations.

The ability to discern whether the other side is genuinely seeking a joint settlement may mean the difference between war and peace. More frequently, keen perception saves time, energy, and resources.

Exercise 1.1

List examples of people at their workplaces (use examples from real life, television, or literature) who try to give the appearance of negotiating with coworkers but who really have no intention of reaching mutual agreement. For each one, what are the motives of that worker? What else does he or she want? What does agreement avoidance do to the atmosphere of the workplace?

Openings come from conquering the resistance to negotiation. To identify opportunities as well as to guard against deceptive or strong-arm measures, it is useful to establish criteria.

There are common obstacles that negotiators must overcome:

- when agreement is not the goal of the parties
- when one party intends to harm or destroy the other
- when one of the negotiators lacks the power to represent his or her party
- when one of the parties is unable or unwilling to submit to reason
- when one of the parties is relatively powerless

Make Agreement the Goal of the Parties

In a marriage, negotiating, renegotiating, redefining the terms of the agreement, and even heated discussions about violations of the agreement may all be healthy signs as long as both mates seek to reach agreement, both realize the other's right to seek an agreed relationship, and both retain their commitment to the importance of the agreement.

When one spouse loses all desire to maintain the relationship, when either one feels justified in making a unilateral decision at the expense of the other, or when either decides that winning is more important than the marriage agreement, whatever relationship remains is sustained by something other than negotiation. For those who have an understanding that terms will be negotiated, repeated violations of the agreement will either end or dramatically alter the relationship.

Similarly, work relationships are not negotiated when parties use the process solely to defeat others or to set up a system in which their side will make all the decisions. In international relations, a negotiated relationship does not exist between two countries when one of the countries covets the other's minerals more than it does an agreement.

Of course, each party wants to get its own way to win, but, to win at all in negotiation, the relationship must be preserved. Kenneth Boulding (1977) uses an example to make the point about subordinating winning to the survival of the relationship:

> In sport, it does not really matter who wins the game, but we have to pretend that it does. If it really mattered, of course, each team would try to poison the beer of the other. If it ever did really matter who won the game, the sport would immediately disintegrate. (pp. 28-29)

In sport and in negotiation, winning must remain subordinate to the "game" or winning does not mean anything.

To create a negotiation opportunity, the advocate for agreement must convince the other side that an agreement will clearly benefit that side's interests and that there are no good alternatives to negotiation.

Confront the Desire to Harm or Destroy

It is often difficult to confront someone who wants to make all the decisions for both sides, but, when domineering paternalism reaches the point where one side seeks to harm or destroy the other, negotiation is impossible. When a relationship between intimate friends degenerates to a point where there is more pleasure in retaliation or more joy in undermining the other's position than in finding a way of living together amicably, the relationship is not a negotiated one. But the exhibition of power does not necessarily prevent negotiations. The distinction is difficult and often subjective.

When management wants to destroy a union or the workers want to sabotage the company, or when a country acts to demolish another, the relationship is not one of negotiation. Legitimate negotiations may include or produce bitterness, militancy, anger, force, pressure, coercion, and resentment. As long as both parties are committed to an agreement with which each can live, the process can be viewed as negotiation.

Pressure is often brought to bear by one side to move the other side into a negotiating posture. One party may apply force as part of a strategy designed to change the perception of the other side during negotiations. For example, in the classical model of collective bargaining, strikes are intended to bring pressure to bear upon an employer, either to push the employer toward a willingness to negotiate or to demonstrate the resolve of the employees on a particular issue.

Certainly, a strike may result in economic hardship to both sides, but, as long as the overall purpose of the pressure is toward an agreement, a negotiation situation still exists. Likewise, lockouts designed specifically to diminish the workers' perception of their own value to the company may not necessarily destroy a negotiating relationship, in spite of the resulting harm.

The crucial point is that a negotiating relationship is possible when both parties have an understanding that the ultimate goal of both is an agreement.

A negotiated relationship is more likely to flourish in an atmosphere of restraint and balance. To fulfill self-interests sometimes requires that one party apply force or pressure on the other side, but a different intention or an unbridled use of that same force may kill the relationship. Some negotiators advocate a "peace through strength" doctrine. They argue, "If I am weak the opposition will exploit that weakness and perhaps avoid negotiating with me at all." As such, the argument makes sense, but some "peace through strength" advocates care more about strength than peace, and in their pursuit of superior strength they really want relationships to be based on their own power, might, and ability to intimidate and not based on an agreement (Komorita, 1977). The application of the "peace through strength" argument breaks down when one asks: "If strengthening one side will be more likely to lead to a peaceful settlement, why is strengthening the other side perceived as a threat?"

In their search for opportunity, negotiators should be wary but not devastated when the other side uses self-promotional propaganda. What do the words and phrases mean? How are they being used? What are the motives? Whether the relationship is personal or professional, it is difficult to understand the motives of the other side. Phrases designed to enhance bargaining power may sound as if they were they designed to destroy negotiations. When one side seeks the destruction of the other side, negotiation is not likely to occur. Negotiators seeking genuine agreement with a recalcitrant opposition must be willing to confront that party and examine their feelings. The negotiators may have to outline steps to rebuild the relationship. They may choose to use their own power tactics, making it easier for the other side to talk than to continue the fight.

Exercise 1.2

Identify an example of some situation in which a person used threats and aggressive speech. Were there any clues that indicated that the aggressor was interested in "defeating" the target? Or did it seem that the aggressor was trying to overcome some insecurity or lack of confidence? Did it appear as if the aggressor wanted to destroy the other person? Or was it an attempt to impress that person or gain some kind of respect?

Attempts to subvert or avoid negotiation do not always take the form of an overt attack. The other form is a covert attempt. A party tries to weaken or destroy the opposition through tactics that include an apparent kindness, care, or paternalism. The artful negotiator is one who can distinguish those who genuinely care and want to help from those who pretend to care just to establish control or those who insist that they know what is best for both sides.

Exercise 1.3

Identify a married couple (one you know from personal experience, television, or literature) that you would characterize as being dominated by one spouse. Does there seem to be any effort on the part of the dominant one to keep the other weak or uncertain? What kind of relationship would you predict there will be in 5 years? Does the couple's behavior pattern prevent genuine negotiation between them?

Whenever others offer to take full responsibility and make all the difficult decisions in the relationship, the negotiator should be more than a little wary of their motives and question why they want to be so helpful. Do they want to keep the negotiator out of the decision-making process? Do they want to keep him or her from developing skills and strengths, or do they simply want to avoid dealing as an equal partner? Identifying and confronting this approach is difficult, but negotiators must clearly and directly express to the other side their suspicions of the relationship and desires for a new type of relationship to build a negotiation opportunity.

Negotiate With Those Who Have the Power to Reach an Agreement

It is not possible to reach an agreement with someone who has no authority to make a valid commitment. The negotiator will want to assess every situation to determine whether the other party has the power to make a decision.

Shoppers who are interested in making careful comparisons may deflect the pressure to make a quick deal and stall an aggressive sales agent by feigning powerlessness. The statements that "I do not have any money," or "I cannot make this kind of decision with consulting my spouse," are ways of saying, "I do not have the power to negotiate." Negotiations cannot take place until the parties have the power to make a decision (Smith, 1988).

A similar stalling tactic is used in labor-management relations. Representatives of management may defer decisions, commitments, or concessions by claiming that they must check with the plant manager or corporate headquarters.

Sometimes the powerlessness is real. Municipal employees who reach accord with the city administration may find the deal vetoed by the city council. Managers who sign a pact with the employees' negotiating team may be frustrated when it is rejected by a vote of the rank and file. When the speaker on one side has no power to speak for his or her side, negotiation does not exist.

With this in mind, someone who wants to avoid negotiation may take steps to weaken or ignore the other team's representatives. For example, companies who want to soften or sidestep a tough militant bargaining team often write letters directly to the rank and file workers or their spouses; they may induce individual workers to defect (Axthelm, 1982); or they may go directly to the public ("An Apology," 1991).

In a similar bypassing gambit, U.S. presidents have tried to circumvent Congress and take their legislative agenda directly to the people. Even when these presidents have won a significant policy victory over Congress, they damaged their future ability to negotiate with members of Congress. When negotiating agents are rendered impotent either because they lack the authority to speak for their side or because they have been bypassed by the opposition, real negotiation will be difficult to achieve.

Exercise 1.4

Identify situations when you felt as if you were "being hassled" or "getting the runaround." Did you sometimes find that the person who was frustrating you did not have any authority to solve your problem or dispute? Could you have settled the matter more easily some other way? Could you have discovered that the other person was in no position to reach an agreement?

Negotiators may be tempted to want to bypass their legitimate counterparts temporarily in an attempt to increase pressure or strike a better deal, but those who seek a genuine agreement will, at some point, need to talk directly with someone who is authorized to represent the other party. Negotiators who face bypassing tactics must be able to muster the support of their constituents and convince the other side that bypassing them will eliminate or reduce the chances for settlement.

Determine What Is Negotiable

To some people, anyone who disagrees with their position is seen as unreasonable. In many cases, the accuser is as unreasonable as the opposition. It is possible to negotiate with people who seem disagreeable or people who sound irrational, as long as they are willing to submit their arguments and evidence to the negotiating table, willing to modify their position, and willing to abide by an agreement. Negotiations do not work when one of the parties will not accept any sense of objective reality or if they are unwilling or unable to subject argument and evidence to any test other than their personal, private opinion.

When one is confronted by an opponent who sincerely makes statements such as these: "I do not care what the facts are" or "I will not ever be convinced by anything," the negotiations are in trouble. A commitment to be unreasonable or an unwillingness to test the case against outside facts or standards obstructs negotiation.

The second kind of irrationality that prevents negotiation is a commitment to dogma. When members of one side argue from dogma, they argue from a set of beliefs and values that are shared with some people and disputed by others. It may not be possible to negotiate an effective resolution resulting in a popularly supported national abortion policy because much of the debate stems from deeply held religious beliefs that participants are unwilling to compromise or reexamine.

Similarly, one cannot negotiate with a terrorist group that will use any means to create a revolution. Dogmatic beliefs do not allow room for discussion, compromise, or a possibility that the other side may be even partly right. Negotiation is impossible with a religious leader or a revolutionary if the former is committed to absolute principles and the latter to absolute change. One worthy person may be committed to preserving traditional values while another honorable individual may seek immediate and drastic structural changes. Each may be brilliant, may be compassionate, and may even be right, but his or her position is not open to negotiation if he or she believes as a matter of faith.

Dogma and doctrine are built on faith and necessarily subjugate reason. Divine, mystical, or otherwise unexplainable doctrine may be right or wrong, but, if it is not subject to human debate, it is not negotiable. Negotiation is a human convention requiring a commitment to rationality from both parties. Within most people, there is a self-defining core that is nonnegotiable. The job of a negotiator is not only to know the part of him- or herself that is not open for compromise but to locate the nonnegotiable core in others as well.

Exercise 1.5

Consider your personal beliefs about what you feel is right or wrong. List five of those beliefs that you are unwilling to compromise. How does your list compare with the lists of others? How can you discover the beliefs or values that others are unwilling to change? If you knew the areas that they would not change and the areas that they might change, how would that influence your discussion with them?

It may not be possible to reach an agreement in some areas with those who will not advance their position to rational scrutiny. For negotiators who seek a genuine agreement with someone who is dogmatic, the most promising path is to focus the talks away from issues that are unchangeable and toward practical, procedural, or methodological questions that may offer common ground.

Build Power to Confront a Strong Opposing Party

Parties do not have to be exactly alike or equal in every way for them to negotiate with each other. A concept such as equality does not lend itself to precise measurement. When comparing the CEO of a major corporation with a popular movie star, it can be argued that one of the individuals is wealthier, better schooled, kinder, nicer looking, and perhaps more intelligent. If one says Norway is as great a country as Brazil, what is the basis for determining equality? Human beings, organizations, countries are multidimensional with an inexhaustible supply of talents, assets, competencies, and disabilities. If the negotiation centers on a border dispute, military might may be an important asset in those talks, but arms may have less impact on deliberations about cultural exchange.

The traditional model for labor-management negotiation has contrasted an economically profitable company and workers without much wealth but with a high economic value to the company. The model works well for negotiation because both parties have the means to meet the needs of the other as well as their own. Both sides can enter negotiations expecting to give and to gain. In that sense, there is a kind of equality at the bargaining table. Deviations from the model contribute to the disintegration of negotiations. The further the parties are from mutual need and mutual gratification, the less likely it is that negotiations will occur. When one side owns a disproportionate share of the economic power, the weaker party may have no choice other than to "cave in." Labor unions throughout the world have a difficult task when they try to confront multinational corporations. Such a corporation has a disproportionate share of the power because of its size and wealth and also its ability to move its operations from one country to another (Reban, 1977).

Rather than accept undesirable settlements, some individuals and groups seek alternatives to negotiation such as violence, sabotage, or assertion of nonnegotiable demands. Weaker parties who feel frustrated may see that a fair settlement is not obtainable, and so they may decide that the destruction of the stronger party is a reasonable goal given the circumstances. Serious inequities nourish the seeds of envy, hatred, revenge, and revolution. Without specific proposals for eliminating major inequities, negotiation has a short life expectancy.

Transforming Obstacles Into Negotiating Opportunities

Even when two sides are engaged in bitter hostilities, seemingly impossible circumstances may be transformed into a situation in which negotiations are possible. Parties outside the conflict can be used to bring pressure to bear on the adversaries and perhaps move them toward negotiation.

The task facing a negotiator with a weak position is to discover some source of power, some weakness in the other side, or some clear, compelling reason to induce the other side to seek agreement.

Negotiators can enhance their opportunities by changing their personal approach to others. Almost everyone will encounter difficult situations and people occasionally, but some individuals seem to have excessive difficulty reaching a good agreement. Individuals without personal credibility cannot be effective negotiators. Persons who yearn to be liked or admired are open for exploitation because their need is so apparent. Those who need to exercise power may have different kinds of problems. After initial successes, people avoid, ignore, or try to discredit them. Clearly, the former group make it too easy for the other side to dictate terms and the latter make it too difficult to obtain an agreement. Gullibility is a trait that negotiators must overcome if they want to turn problems into potential. Accepting the other side's apparent motives as genuine may put the negotiator at a serious disadvantage. Negotiators who are strong and perceptive can decide whether to withdraw from a dishonest relationship or to confront the deception.

Negotiators can look for opportunities to negotiate by understanding the experiences, needs, and motivations of the other side. People who have had previous bad experiences with "negotiation" may be reluctant to enter into the process again. Michael Terry (1977) studied British workers' avoidance of formal contract language covering work practices. Many of them resisted formalizing of the rules; they were more confident in their ability to handle the informal rules of workplace practice. They feared that managers who were skillful with contract language would succeed in formalizing only the practices that benefited themselves. They worried that rigid contract rules would rob workers of any discretionary power. The workers resisted formal negotiation because they did not see it as profitable. A skilled negotiator could either use the informal process to reach agreement or could offer the appropriate reassurances to bring the disaffected back into formal negotiations.

On a practical level, negotiations are time consuming, costly, often unpleasant, and the outcome may not be desirable. Unilateral decision making gives the deciding party a sense of control and flexibility. Until both sides are willing to accept a bipartisan solution, talks may occur but not negotiations (Baldwin, 1976).

In long-term bilateral relationships, negotiators will want to argue that negotiation is good for all concerned and avoiding negotiation may lead to problems for everyone. The weaker side will eventually tire of living under someone else's terms and of not having a choice. As long as the dominant side has any need for the subordinate party, it must continue to make concessions (to people who seem hostile and ungrateful); it must bear the burden and the expense of regulating the behavior of the subordinate party; it must bear full responsibility for the decision making of both parties; and it must be prepared for the eventual resentment, resistance, and retaliation of the subordinate party.

Exercise 1.6

Identify a "boss" (in fact or fiction) who makes unilateral decisions. Identify some of the short-term and long-term advantages and disadvantages for the boss who uses this approach.

Even in circumstances when an agreement would be good for both sides, the animosity may be so great that the parties need a prenegotiation phase before they even try to pursue an agreement. Mediator Harold H. Saunders (1985) used experiences with Middle East countries to build a five-stage prenegotiation model:

1. Identify and define issues or conflicts.
2. Secure a commitment from both sides to negotiate a settlement.
3. Arrange location and general proceedings of the negotiations.
4. Create the environment for visible negotiations.
5. Seek methods that will provide for implementation.

When the parties are unable or unwilling to discuss substantial issues that separate them, successes at "negotiating" procedure may be necessary before real issues can be discussed. Many times, one of the parties will not negotiate without heavy pressure. Nostalgics who long for the "good old days" and traditional authority often view negotiation as weak, compromising, and morally questionable. Individuals who always expect others to grant them favorable terms find negotiating disappointing. Those who resent any obligation to meet and discuss an issue or problem dislike negotiation because they prefer to make unilateral decisions. They may attempt to subvert, bypass, or overpower the other party rather than negotiate. They place little faith in negotiation. At the other extreme are those who deny any role for tradition and authority. They may insist that every conflict be open for "negotiation" as they seem to believe that it is possible to negotiate anything (Ways, 1979). They place too much faith in negotiation processes; they often expect others to want what they want; they burden those processes with trivia and with matters that could be swiftly and justly settled another way. They, too, subvert honest negotiations.

Finally, there are those who simply use meetings as an opportunity to fill a void in their personal lives or just waste a little time. As a practical matter, they may never reach a useful agreement.

To create opportunities for mutual gain, negotiators must always be ready to demonstrate that negotiation offers the best possibilities for mutually beneficial relationships. Because, however, there are those who seek the short-term advantages to be gained by merely pretending to negotiate, there are many kinds of interaction that are not negotiation. Genuine negotiation possibilities exist when both sides have the desire, the opportunity, and the capability of reaching an agreement. If these criteria are not met, those sincerely interested in negotiation can decide whether to abandon the relationship or to transform it into one in which negotiation is possible.

Exercise 1.7

Many exchanges between people look like negotiations even though genuine negotiation does not actually occur. Scan a weekly newsmagazine or a Sunday newspaper. Try to find examples of conflicts in relationships that are characterized by each of the following:

- agreement is not the goal of the parties
- one party intends to harm or destroy the other
- one of the negotiators lacks the power to represent his or her party
- one of the parties is unable or unwilling to submit to reason
- one of the parties is relatively powerless

Develop a strategy for overcoming the obstacle and creating a negotiation opportunity.

Improving Perception

The magic, mystery, and challenge of negotiation stem from the unknown factors. If people had complete knowledge of themselves, the other side, and the issues, negotiations would be far different than we know them to be. Because that is not the case, there is an excitement about the processes of negotiating. Trying to understand one's own needs and capabilities, or another's expectations and motivations, and trying to set realistic levels for reaching agreement all require skill and patience. Improvement of one's perceptual skills is possible and desirable. Perceptions are important in negotiation because they form the basis for all of the moves made.

The first perceptual challenge is to develop an accurate view of oneself. A reasonably accurate self-perception is difficult to attain because the human mind has mechanisms that allow people to block or overlook emotionally painful experiences. These "self-deception" mechanisms make it possible for individuals to function without full self-awareness. The mind allows individuals to reduce pain, doubt, and irritations of everyday life, but in doing so it also limits and otherwise distorts self-perceptions. Generally, people do not fully acknowledge and effectively evaluate information about themselves, especially if it seems unpleasant or disagreeable (Goleman, 1985). Accurate self-perception permits the pain that is otherwise blocked by self-deception. Though individuals who are able to get a full and honest look at themselves may not like what they see, an accurate self-perception is needed during negotiations. A distorted self-perception could make the negotiator vulnerable to flattery, intimidation, or other kinds of manipulation.

Accurate self-knowledge is a requirement for good negotiating, but it is also useful for negotiators to see themselves as other see them. To a great extent, the way that negotiators view their role influences what they do and how well they do. For example, negotiators who have a positive orientation (i.e., see themselves as seeking to obtain gains) are more flexible, concessionary, and likely to reach a higher outcome compared with those who have a negative orientation (see themselves as defending against losses). Those who have a realistic self-confidence are much more flexible, concessionary, and achieve more than those who are overconfident (Neale & Bazerman, 1985b).

Negotiators also need to view their relationships with others accurately. The evidence shows that individuals who are oriented toward teamwork are able to reach higher joint payoffs in negotiation than those who are oriented toward achieving individual goals (Schulz & Pruitt, 1978). Negotiators who have not thought about themselves, their image, and their role have less control over negotiations. A negotiator who has a self-image that differs sharply from the image that others see is not likely to be effective. Knowing oneself and one's role allows for a more accurate assessment of personal power and helps to reduce the chances for the other side to exploit any vulnerabilities.

Empathy is possible without agreement. An accurate understanding of the other side is useful. By projecting distorted motives, perhaps falsely assuming that the other side intends harm, negotiators are likely to make poor decisions. At a minimum, negotiators need to be able to say, "I understand what you are saying and I see why you are taking that position, but I disagree with it." A more sophisticated negotiator will mentally allow the other side's position to challenge his or her own. Rather than simply dismissing the other side and seeking evidence to prove the error of their position, this more sophisticated approach will allow their position a fuller kind of consideration. If the others are right, that could be a good reason for the negotiator to change his or her mind. But if, after this process, the negotiator has seen little compelling evidence from the other side, he or she should have much stronger arguments and evidence.

While negotiators often do not know the other side's position very well, few negotiators seem to have any idea of the strategy that the other side is trying to employ. In simulations, negotiators have great difficulty discriminating among opposition strategies, which included "competing," "avoiding," "compromising," "accommodating," or "collaborating" (Duane, Azevedo, & Anderson, 1985). If a negotiator does not have a clear assessment of the other side, or an accurate idea of its strategy, he or she will not have prepared a good plan of counterstrategies to employ, and the other side will be well positioned to take significant advantage.

The perception of the negotiation process plays a major role in shaping the outcome. Those who see negotiations as a kind of war are likely to achieve a different result than those who see it as a joint exploration for mutually beneficial options. Those with a clear perception of the issues and a realistic expectation of a settlement will negotiate differently than those who hold great expectations.

Perceptions and expectations are shaped by one's environment. Family, friends, and coworkers influence the way an individual approaches negotiations, and environmentally induced factors set limits and blinders on what negotiators see. Poor perception can lead to unnecessary risks, to passivity, to bad proposals, to impasses, and to inappropriate agreements. One may not eliminate deception entirely, but it is possible to reduce it and improve perception dramatically. Thorough preparation—which includes deep, honest probing of oneself, one's opposition, and the issues— helps. Additionally, negotiators can adopt specific attitudes and behaviors to promote clear and accurate perception:

1. Negotiators want to hear what the other side has to say. Negotiators who force themselves to listen, to seek out the other side's main ideas and supporting evidence, are imposing a self-discipline and organization that can keep them from missing important messages.

2. They seek a positive relationship with the other side. This should promote a better quality of messages and keep both sides from developing a negative mind-set unnecessarily or prematurely.

3. They work to solve the conflict. To solve the problem, one makes a commitment to negotiate and to look for solutions. The negotiator's focus is aimed at opportunities. Those who look for ways to continue the conflict will almost always find them.

4. They seek an appropriate communication environment. The ideal time and place are those where both sides can talk with each other without distractions, where each side is comfortable and each feels that the other side has no particular advantage. Many negotiation sessions would benefit from shorter meetings and more breaks.

5. They respect the adversaries as speakers for their cause. Treat adversaries as a valued resource that contributes to a realistic perception. Respect should not be offered as a benefit to the other side but used as a tool to increase accurate information and to seek opportunities for agreement.

6. They encourage the free flow of information and promote the full exchange of diverse ideas during preparation. Encourage a devil's advocate. The diversity of ideas should increase the number of options.

7. They entertain the idea that they are wrong. If they are, what are the likely consequences? Could they be partly wrong? Does their position lend itself to alteration or compromise?

Confronted by people who hold opinions different than theirs, negotiators have a range of options. They can change their minds. They can try to change the other's mind. They can change their behavior. They can try to change the other's behavior. They can set more realistic terms. They can evaluate the other person's reality. They can set their proposals in new and perhaps more appropriate terms. They can effectively analyze the other person's proposals. They can berate the other person or try to understand them. Negotiators who have a clear understanding of themselves, the other side, and the issues enjoy more choices and better choices than those who have less complete or less accurate information.

EXERCISE GUIDE

The moral of Tim and Abdul's story at the beginning of the chapter: Abdul is not in a good position to work out a mutually satisfactory solution with Tim. Before genuine negotiations can take place, Tim needs to be convinced that negotiations are necessary and that he will somehow be better off with a negotiated relationship. Abdul needs to develop confidence and establish himself as one who should be taken seriously. He needs to push his hostilities aside and analyze what specific terms he wants to achieve and what problems he wants to eliminate. Finally, before genuine negotiations can occur, Abdul will need to determine his own power in the relationship. He may want to find out what kinds of changes Tim would like from him, and he needs to know what kinds of appeals are likely to be effective with Tim.

EXERCISE 1.1 Many people try to give an appearance of cooperation and democratic decision making at work. They may want to appear egalitarian and considerate, but they still prefer to do things their way. Some may be afraid of agreement-seeking processes because they fear change; others, because they lack confidence in their ability to reach a desirable settlement; and others perhaps simply do not want to take the time and effort to negotiate.

These pseudonegotiators are likely to demonstrate excellent short-term performance but probably contribute to an atmosphere of suspicion and distrust over any length of time.

EXERCISE 1.2 Many examples of aggressive behavior seem to be designed to impress others or to build self-confidence. Although, in some cases, aggressive people are exhibiting a passion for their cause and may be eager to enter into discussions about it.

EXERCISE 1.3 The discussion should examine whether dominant-submissive relationships work and if they are likely to work for a long-term relationship. The dominant party may make the decisions but is responsible for them and for enforcing them. The submissive partner does not have as much responsibility but loses personal identity and preferences. The relationship does not foster negotiation and may not even permit it to occur.

EXERCISE 1.4 Discussion should focus on methods of detecting whether a person has the power to reach an agreement. Methods include locating the formal decision maker within the relevant organization, but some attention should be devoted to informal (actual) decision makers such as secretaries, aides, and deputies.

EXERCISE 1.5 Most people would believe that murder, robbery, and lying are wrong, and perhaps that democracy and certain individual freedoms are right. Is there any ambiguity in the beliefs? Are any areas of compromise possible? What are the issues that are beyond compromise?

EXERCISE 1.6 The discussion should examine the advantages and disadvantages of making decisions and then imposing those decisions on others. The "boss" gains flexibility and, if he or she has enough power, subordinates will do what the boss wants. But "bosses'" unilateral decisions are restricted by their own limited perspectives and may be resisted or sabotaged by subordinates.

EXERCISE 1.7 Discussion should focus on the obstacles but also on the kinds of changes that need to occur to make a genuine negotiating opportunity.

Identifying and Pursuing
Useful Negotiating Goals

The Story of Linda and Steve's Decision to Adopt a Pet

Married for less than a year, Linda and Steve live in a small house with a large fenced-in backyard. Linda teaches nights at a community college and spends most days working at home preparing for classes. Steve's job keeps him in the office during weekdays and requires him to make overnight trips 4-6 times a month. The big advantage of their schedules is that at least once a month they are able to take a long weekend traveling together. The disadvantage is that they each spend more time home alone than they like. They both love their work and plan to postpone having children for at least 5 years.

What they both want right now is a pet, or at least they think that they do. They each grew up with pets. Steve has fond memories of his loyal childhood German shepherd. Steve feels that he would worry less during his nights away from home knowing that there was a big dog at home with Linda. Steve does not relate to cats well and thinks that he might even be allergic to them.

Linda was raised with both dogs and cats. She likes both as long as they are small cuddly creatures. Linda figures that she will probably have more of the responsibility for the pet simply because she spends more time at home. Because there are times when no one is home, she thinks that maybe a cat would handle the solitary periods better. On their trips to the shopping mall, they stop for a look at the pet store. Linda is inevitably drawn to the little kittens and Steve heads for the big dogs. Other than agreeing that they would like a pet and each expressing mild preferences, they have not discussed the matter much.

Linda and Steve can probably reach an agreement with each other on this issue. They each need to decide what they want, why they want it, what they would find acceptable, and what they will do if they cannot agree.

Careless individuals make up their negotiating goals as they proceed. "I think I will go talk with the salesman and see what kind of deal I can make" is not the best consumer approach. The odds in this situation favor the seller. Easy goals are not likely to produce significant gains either. Tough but realistic goals, a belief in those goals, and confidence in the ability to achieve the goals are factors in successful negotiation (Huber & Neale, 1986).

Setting goals is a way of pointing toward achievement. The goal-setting process also helps to sort out what is more desired and what is less desired. That process should function as the framework for making important distinctions and decisions about when to compromise and when to hold fast. As Zemke (1980) summarized: "The would-be negotiator must believe that his or her best interests and those of the organization or persons that he or she represents in a negotiation situation . . . are best served by holding fast to long-term objectives and dancing the compromise waltz with short-term needs and wants" (p. 28).

In other words, negotiators need major objectives that are clear enough to function as a stabilizing force and general guide. They also need goals flexible enough to allow them give-and-take on issues that do not compromise their overall purpose.

The daily environment conditions many people to be passive and accept whatever they are given. For many, trying to figure out what they really want is difficult. The following steps should help create useful goals:

1. Define the negotiating situation or the problem.
2. Investigate history and previous attempts at resolution.
3. Picture the best imaginable deal and the worst acceptable deal.

4. Identify supporters and opponents.
5. Estimate alternatives to an agreement.

Define the Negotiating Situation or Problem

Following these simple steps means having already completed a more thorough preparation than most negotiators. Those who prepare to this point should have a reasonable idea of what they want to accomplish and probably a reasonable estimate of what they can expect.

Simple questions and problems of everyday life are often the basis of conflict and often form the rationale for many social and commercial transactions. Someone looking for housing may ask the following questions: Do I want to buy a condo or a single family dwelling? Do I have the time or resources to maintain a large living area? Will I have full responsibility for cleaning it? How much can I afford to pay?

For those who decide immediately to buy a condominium, and have identified a particular one, the negotiation problem may be that "they need to get their dream for the right price." On the other hand, there are others who are looking for a place to live and a condo came to mind because they have always lived in a condo. Their problem is more broadly defined: "finding a new place to live that fits their needs, desires, and budget."

In a different kind of example, one of the frequently reported work-related complaints is that the temperature in the workplace is too hot or too cold. At first glance, it seems like a problem that requires only an adjustment of the thermostat, but reaching an agreeable solution to this problem is often complicated. Some operations require temperatures that are too cold for human comfort; or sometimes essential machinery may produce heat that feels unbearable; sometimes workers cannot agree on a desirable temperature. Is the negotiation issue whether to raise or lower the temperature? Is it how to redesign and rebuild the work site? Is it whether to seek a transfer to another work site? Is it to reach an agreement about an equitable procedure for controlling the temperature or a method for deciding who will work in the undesirable setting?

To use another example, family members who share the same living quarters often disagree about the distribution of housework. In response to a perception of inequity, several questions might be examined: "What kind of change do I want?" "Are my goals to get my spouse or children to do more?" "Is the problem that I do not seem to have time to do everything I need to do?" "Maybe the problem is not housework but a symptom of some stronger tension within the family relationship?" "Can the family agree on a common definition of what housework means?" It may be surprising to find that one spouse who does not cook wants to classify cooking as a hobby rather than housework, while the other does not regard the hours spent in the garden or washing the car as housework.

Generally, when people search for goals, they want to negotiate an immediate solution but the preferred goal is less direct (Burton, 1987). One alternative is to negotiate for personal respect, esteem, or reputation. The goal is to seek a more positive relationship with the other party rather than any specific solution to a specific problem. This goal is necessary when the negotiator is not in a position to solve specific problems until a more equitable relationship is achieved.

Another alternative is a dispute resolution process. Here too, rather than solving the particular problem, the goal of the parties is to negotiate the method that will be used to resolve problems as they arise in the future.

Using the example about sharing housework, rather than negotiating over who will do what, a couple might negotiate a more equal relationship, or they might focus on the process for doing chores. The process might look something like this: (a) They will jointly create a list of chores to be done each Saturday; (b) each will alternately pick a chore from the list; (c) the first pick will be awarded to the winner of a coin toss; (d) each will be responsible for accomplishing the chores on his or her list; (e) chores left uncompleted will remain the responsibility of the person who selected them (if left undone, they will not reappear on the list of shared chores next Saturday).

Honesty, positive expectations, and precision are key qualities for defining the problem or conflict. Negotiators who realistically assess what they need, want, and expect have a better opportunity for satisfaction than those who fool themselves. Neale and Bazerman (1985b) found that those who expect positive results are more likely to pursue negotiations than those who see their goal as guarding against a loss.

Finally, precise goals serve the negotiator's interests. Those who are able to quantify the levels they intend to reach perform better than their counterparts with more general goals (Hermone, 1974). Negotiators who have an easy issue and a relationship that provides open, honest discussion want to ask their counterpart to create a separate definition of the conflict or problem. Each should try to think about the problem from every perspective. At this point, none of the possibilities should be eliminated. They may be able to agree on a working definition of the problem, even as they stay open to new possibilities.

Exercise 2.1

You are the owner and plant manager of a small steel fabricating shop employing 50 people with whom you must negotiate a new contract. While your product line has remained predictable over the past few years, you make about 50% of your annual profit on products that are "last minute" special orders. These special orders also create a large amount of scrap. In the past few months, your material costs have risen sharply, and the outlook is for even higher price increases. You know that you cannot continue to pass along the higher costs to your customers. They already complain that your special order prices are far too high. There is a new process that will help you recover scrap, but it is very expensive and will not be cost effective if the material prices stabilize. In your last labor negotiations 3 years ago, you succeeded in keeping wage increases low even as you continued to maintain a very high net profit. The workers are expecting a substantial increase in wages and benefits this time. You have a month's inventory on your regular product line, but even a short strike could hurt your special order business. Identify and analyze your negotiating problem.

History and Previous Attempts at Resolution

Many times, negotiators treat their problems as new and unique, but most of the problems undertaken have some useful history.

Those who discover the failures or successes of past resolutions may learn something useful for treating the current conflict. Negotiators will want to know when the problem began. Did it happen at once or develop over time? Who were the people involved? Were they aligned with a particular side? How did the disputants at the beginning see the problem? Has it changed over time? Have people on both sides of the issue lost interest in it? Have they forgotten about it? Or have both sides become more firmly entrenched in their own positions?

A history of the dispute should give some clues about how to proceed. Perhaps the sides might be tired of the dispute and wish to work on a settlement. Maybe a particular person who had a major part in continuing the dispute has had a change of heart or a change in position. Maybe organizational pressures have changed for one side, making them willing to reexamine the issue. The history of the dispute may even suggest that now is not the best time to try for a settlement.

In one-time negotiations, one can try to find out how the other party has responded in similar situations or at least the likely response. Negotiators should never feel locked into the patterns of the past, but they should be familiar with the past.

Exercise 2.2

An extremist political group that has been holding several U.S. citizens hostage for more than 2 years has recently sent signals to the U.S. government that it is now willing to talk. You have been asked to represent the United States in those talks. What steps would you take to learn the history that is relevant to the dispute? What will you want to know?

Picture the Best Imaginable Deal and the Worst Acceptable Deal

For those who are led by their dreams and cautioned by their common sense, negotiating can have a big payoff. Imagining the ideal solution provides a strong sense of direction. The vision of the ideal solution also gives negotiators a chance to attain a better settlement. Possibly the initial proposals will appeal to the other side or coincide with their interests.

Some negotiators make a mistake because they stray from their own personal desires and try too hard to please the other side. For example, many husbands and wives have an agreement that a joint discussion is expected before either makes an expensive purchase. If the wife is especially concerned with saving money, the husband may try to accommodate by identifying a less desirable but less expensive brand and try to convince her by showing the savings when compared with other brands. Even if the money-conscious wife agrees, the expenditure is likely to cause her to feel some level of resentment. The shopping husband is likely to feel some dissatisfaction because he did not buy the quality he really wanted, and his purchase is still resented.

In situations where one person tries to represent the interests of the other rather than his or her own interest, neither side will have a good opportunity for self-satisfaction. Negotiators who pursue what they really want may not always attain it, but they might, and the other side might be as happy with the result.

Still, negotiators who remain starry-eyed optimists are not especially productive. Common sense, a knowledge of the real world, and an understanding of the other party help to keep the goals realistic, make the negotiator more credible, and may contribute to a smoother transaction. A clear understanding of the best deal imaginable points the negotiator in the proper direction, just as a clear understanding of the least desired acceptable settlement keeps one from being forced, sweet-talked, or tricked into an unsatisfactory agreement.

Exercise 2.3

You drive a gas-guzzling car with 142,000 miles on the odometer. You live in a hot climate. Your air conditioner is broken and you drive 30 miles each way to work everyday. Your bumper sticker reads: "Don't Laugh It's Paid For," but you don't laugh either because you spend too much for gas and you know that large repair bills are not far off. Make a best- and a worst-case scenario for deciding whether to buy a new car.

Identify the Supporters and Opponents

There is a certain comfort when there is a clear distinction between those on one side and those on the other. In commerce, the seller and the buyer usually seem to be on opposite sides. Mostly they are, but on rare occasions their goals are identical and the real negotiating is with a third party. A home buyer may agree with the seller on price, condition of the property, and a timetable for possession only to find a conflict with the lending institutions, who will not give the terms needed for the mortgage, or maybe it is the appraiser who frustrates both buyer and seller with a list of changes that must be made before the transaction can be completed.

The process that occurs when labor unions push for a contract with management is popularly pictured as a struggle between two monolithic forces. That image is not accurate: There are workers who will oppose some of the union proposals and there are managers who overtly oppose the union but secretly hope that the union succeeds in securing major increases in pensions and insurance benefits because they know that managers will receive the same increases. When a large organization negotiates, there is a likelihood that internal factions will actively oppose or quietly undermine their own representatives. Former U.S. Secretary of Labor John Dunlop (1984) argues: "In two-party negotiations, it takes an agreement within each side to make an agreement across the table, that is, it take three agreements to reach one" (p. 21).

Supporters and opponents do not always come in predictable patterns. It should be easy to identify likely supporters from within the group, among personal friends, and from those who oppose the other side. Knowing who will be likely to agree and who will likely oppose gives the negotiator some indication of what particular individuals are interested in achieving and possibly what it will take to reach a settlement.

Exercise 2.4

You want to quit work and return to school to finish a course of study you started a few years ago. You talked with a counselor and learned you can graduate within one year. While this

will certainly create a burden for your family, it will lead to much higher pay within 3 to 5 years. Identify those likely to be your supporters and those likely to oppose within your family.

Estimate the Alternatives to an Agreement

When two parties reach a mutually agreeable pact, the result is often a settlement that works well for both sides. Frequently, however, one side cannot get the other side to negotiate. When negotiations look as if they will be difficult, negotiators will want to plan contingencies in case they should fail to reach an agreement. Roger Fisher and William Ury (1981), of the Harvard Negotiating Project, refer to this process as "knowing your BATNA," the "Best Alternative to a Negotiated Agreement" (p. 104).

Three major reasons for including this step are as follows:

1. Negotiators who have a viable alternative to a negotiated settlement have a greater sense of bargaining power. Even with a desire for reaching agreement, a contingency plan allows greater independence from the other side.
2. A concrete alternative provides the negotiator with a reference for measuring the viability of the other side's proposals.
3. The alternative plan to a negotiated settlement should help negotiators realistically evaluate their own proposals and expectations.

Different types of relationships produce different levels of alternatives. For example, in most commercial transactions, there are usually good alternatives. In most cases, consumers who cannot reach an agreeable settlement with a particular seller will simply look for another, look for a substitute product or service, or postpone the purchase. In labor contract negotiations, workers may decide that they will work under an extension of the old contract rather than settle for an undesirable contract. Friends or lovers who lose their ability to reach agreement with each other seem to have less than ideal alternatives, but, even in difficult situations, knowing that alternatives exist and knowing what they are help to put the negotiations in proper perspective.

Exercise 2.5

You have lived away from your hometown for 5 years; you and your family want to move back. The economy back home is not good and after a long search you have found only one job lead. You think they will offer you the job but at a wage that is much lower than you make now and lower than you think you need to live comfortably. How would you identify alternatives to reaching a satisfactory wage agreement with your prospective employer?

As part of setting goals and estimating alternatives, it is necessary to listen and learn the goals and priorities of the other side (Greenhalgh, Neslin, & Gilkey, 1985). An understanding of the counterpart's goals helps to establish power in an adversarial environment or build cooperation in a collaborative one.

Listening Actively

Active listening is important for identifying and creating negotiating goals, because listening helps to orient the negotiator to the environment. When they listen, negotiators have an opportunity to learn about the other parties, the issues, and the situation. The key is to listen for needs on the other side, for opportunities to meet those needs, and for ways to adapt proposals to the needs of the other side. Listeners gain bargaining power; talkers often exhaust it. Because people do not learn much while they are talking, negotiators should attempt to talk less than 50% of the time (Byrnes, 1987).

In negotiation, there are four major reasons to listen:

1. to discover the needs of constituents and teammates;
2. to learn the other side's proposals and strengths;
3. to discern subtle position changes and openings; and
4. to show the other side that their proposals are understood.

Though self-explanatory, neither of the first two objectives is easy to accomplish. Misunderstandings occur even in the best communication circumstances. Zemke (1980) found that good paraphrasing skills help to produce better listening results in negotiation. The act of repeating back the other side's general statement reduces misunderstanding but it also imposes a valuable discipline on the listener.

Listening for the subtle signs from the other side requires the same sharp concentration, but the payoffs are high for those who understand the message hidden in the speaker's words. Speakers who take a hard line may find it nearly impossible to admit that they were wrong. Negotiators who are alert and sensitive to small signals showing a shifting position are in a position to find agreements.

When the talks become personal, negotiators tend to rationalize their behavior and justify their positions, even as they project undesirable characteristics on the other side. Hostilities can harden because each side has difficulty retreating from the harsh accusations and characterizations it has made. To break these patterns, it may take someone who can carefully listen for minuscule movement in the position of the other side. Those who have learned to listen well can make great contributions to reaching agreement.

The last major reason for active listening is that it demonstrates to members of the other side that the negotiator has a strong desire to know what they are saying. This holds true whether negotiations are friendly or hostile, intimate or formal. It is desirable for the other side to see that the negotiator is listening. Good listening helps to promote greater communication from the other side (Gouray, 1987).

In addition to the other substantial gains, listening and the image of being a good listener have an interpersonal payoff. Johnson (1971) found that negotiators respond to warmth and empathy of listening behavior with reciprocal feelings. Accurate restatement of the negotiator's position produces a greater willingness to reach agreement. Listening behavior can demonstrate a sense of both understanding and caring to the other side.

Good listening skills are useful for discovering the needs of constituents, for understanding the case that the other side is presenting, for detecting subtle movement in the other side, and for demonstrating a sense of understanding and concern to them.

Here are a few guidelines that, if put into practice, can produce immediate results:

1. Actively listen. Pay attention to what the other side is saying. Listeners who can push their mind to anticipate, to seek, to summarize the main points often know the speaker's case better than he or she does.

2. Avoid judgments. No matter what the negotiator thinks about the other side, there should be an attempt to suspend judgment until the complete statement is heard. Judging a speaker does not help or hurt the speaker as much as it distorts the information that the listener receives. Early judgments hurt the listener.

3. Disregard distractions. There are so many things that take one's mind away from the message. Outside sights and sounds, disruptions, discomfort, shock, disgust, boredom, and lack of clarity all work to destroy the concentration on the speaker's main points. Good listeners lose concentration too, but, unlike poor listeners, they are able to regain it.

4. Listen for ideas rather than facts. Facts are important, but out of context they are useless and distracting. A thorough understanding of the main idea puts the listener in a position to evaluate the meaning of each fact and decide how much weight to give it.

5. Outline the main ideas. Good listeners do not wait for the information to come to them. Listening occurs faster than speaking so listeners can productively engage their minds using the extra time to summarize and reorganize the speaker's main points. A listener who masters this skill often has a better grasp of the speaker's message than the speaker does. Paraphrasing the message back to the speaker may offer opportunities for settlement that would not otherwise exist.

6. Interrupt and probe. The popular image of a good listener is someone quiet, polite, and passive. Good listeners do not often fit that description. They follow up. They may interrupt the speaker to get clarification. They may make a speaker uncomfortable, especially one who has little to say. But speakers who care about transmitting their messages accurately usually welcome an attentive listener.

It is not difficult to become a good listener, quickly. By wanting to improve, following a few guidelines, and practicing active listening at every opportunity, a person can develop excellent skills.

EXERCISE GUIDE

The moral of Linda and Steve's story at the beginning of the chapter: Steve and Linda need to decide separately and then jointly what kind of animal companionship they want. In setting goals, they need to consider the kinds of characteristics they seek as well as their willingness to accommodate the needs of the pet. They should consider what the addition of the pet will do to their family dynamics. Because Steve and Linda love each other, the danger is that Steve might agree to adopt a cat because he thinks it will make Linda happy, or Linda may propose adopting a big dog simply because she thinks that's what Steve wants. Their chance of success increases if they know their own interests and then work toward joint goals.

EXERCISE 2.1 A manager who faces pressure to increase performance or make unpopular changes should clearly define what the employees are being asked to do. The negotiating goal should consider whether or not the other side will see the request as reasonable or necessary. In this case, the owner/manager may construct a goal that will make some short-term demands on employees in exchange for long-term security and mutual profit, or he may present the choices to the employees and seek their involvement in identifying and solving the problem.

EXERCISE 2.2 The search for pertinent information should include the history of the dispute, the disputing parties, and the previous attempts at resolution. The negotiator will want to know about the reasons for past failures as well as the changes in the issue, in the parties, or in the circumstances that would create a new possibility for resolution.

EXERCISE 2.3 A major part of the goal-construction process should be an examination of the consequence of achieving one's goal. In this case, faced with two extreme options, the would-be negotiator should consider best-case and worst-case scenarios for buying a new car or hanging on to the old junker.

EXERCISE 2.4 The discussion should focus on the effects of the decision on each family member, the kinds of issues that would influence their positions, and the kinds of appeals that would be effective with each one.

EXERCISE 2.5 The major choices are moving or not moving. There are, however, a range of options within each choice. Are there some changes that would make staying more attractive? Would it be possible to stay for a little while and wait for the economy to revive? Would it be desirable to move closer to your hometown? Is it desirable to accept a low-paying job as a temporary move to put you in contact with other jobs in your hometown? Is it likely that the job offered will develop into an acceptable job soon?

Finding and Using Information

*The Story of Jerry and Lisa's
Attempt at a Happy Vacation*

The rush to finish school, a quick wedding, and the beginning of two careers have not allowed Jerry and Lisa any block of free time. They have never had a vacation that lasted more than an extended weekend. Now they have a big opportunity. They both have vacation time available the last two weeks in August and they want to make the most of the time. Another factor in the decision-making process is their desire to have a child in the next few years; they feel that this may be their last chance to be alone like this for years.

They have two major conflicts. Lisa sees vacation as a chance to get away from a hectic work schedule. Her vision includes a deserted beach, no clocks, few people, and no plans. Jerry is ready to bust loose from the restrictions of a small office. He pictures a trip to a big city with museums and nightlife, or maybe a week of hiking and biking.

The other conflict is about money. Lisa wants a simple, quiet vacation, in part because she wants to save money, or at least not spend too much. Jerry thinks that a vacation is the time to "live it up." He is picturing Paris or Rio de Janeiro. Her vision is a nearby beach. They agree that this is a great opportunity and that they need to get away. They have not yet begun to make plans or even check out possible destinations.

Lisa and Jerry can probably reach an agreement and each have a satisfying vacation. They need to make their individual goals and interests more concrete. What kinds of information

35

should they each seek? Should they look for information individually or jointly? How should they use the information as they discuss the issue together?

Some of the major questions that each side faces during negotiations are these: "What will the other side settle for?" "How much will I have to give up to get what I want or need?" "How far can I push the other side before I damage or break the relationship?" Those who possess very specific information are able to make a close estimate of the answers. That estimating ability translates into power. Shrewd negotiators can take advantage of their counterparts' misperception or lack of information.

In buyer and seller negotiation, sellers have a significant advantage, resulting in measurably higher prices when they are given relevant information not available to the buyer (Chatterjee & Lilien, 1984). Negotiators who find new information showing a strength for their side or a weakness on the other side have discovered something useful.

Exercise 3.1

If you are a union negotiator seeking wage increases from a company who firmly insists on granting no wage increases, what types of information would you like to discover to use in your discussions with the company? What types of information would strengthen their case against you? What single piece of information would prevent you from striking?

Negotiators can use information more productively for their own interests and still make the process work smoothly. In general, when both sides talk to each other and exchange information, the results tend to be better for both than in situations where sides retain and guard their own information (Daniels, 1967). The process of giving and receiving information moves bargainers toward more realistic aspirations.

Negotiators who receive new information during negotiations tend to move away from extreme positions (Jennings, Paulson, &

Williamson, 1987). Negotiators who are knowledgeable about the process and the consequences are more reasonable in their initial position and in their final position and more likely to grant concessions to close an agreement (DeNisi & Dworkin, 1981). Those who expect too little raise their expectations when they receive relevant information, while those with excessively high initial expectations tend to lower them in the process (Hamner & Harnett, 1975). Information is potent, but it is seldom used as effectively as it could be. The power of information is often overrated and underrated at the same time.

It is overrated by those who think it has a transforming magical power. They tend to think, "If we just had more information . . . ," or "We have to provide them with exact information to change their minds." Those who are awed by information seem certain that, if they had better information, it would almost certainly provide better decisions and agreements. They are only partly right. Every day, people have access to information that can help improve their health, increase their wealth, or contribute to their happiness. Because information is hardly ever complete or totally accurate, however, it gets buried, ignored, or discredited. But even correct and complete information does not necessarily contribute to the best outcome. Often it is seen as suspicious or as an additional source of worry.

Exercise 3.2

You and your spouse are moving to a big city because you have a spectacular job there. You prefer to live in the city close to work and other conveniences, while your spouse prefers a tranquil suburb away from the hurried pace of the city. What kinds of information do you seek from him or her? From other sources? What kinds of information do you try to provide?

To a great extent, the way information is used depends on the orientation of the negotiator. Those who see the negotiation as a complex puzzle are more likely to overrate information than those who see the negotiations as a simple, straightforward exercise, yet those with the complex orientation also have greater tolerance for uncertainty and are better able to predict the likely outcome of the negotiation than those with the simple orientation (Streufert, Streufert, & Castore, 1968). As the twenty-first century arrives, so much information is available that

1. any particular piece of information is likely to be lost or overwhelmed in the sheer volume;
2. much of the information provided is deliberately biased or incomplete, presented to make a sale, gain a vote, or seek help;
3. some information is inconsistent with what people want to know or believe and so they tend to discount it;
4. even well-informed people spend their information gathering time inefficiently (How many times does one see the same selected facts from the same news story repeated on TV, radio, newspapers, magazines?); and
5. it is difficult to determine how information is to be evaluated and used.

In an examination of the continuing debate about gun control, pro-gun groups provide information that suggests guns are useful in protecting against intrusions into the home. On the other hand, advocates of gun restrictions cite studies that show that the presence of guns in a house increases the likelihood a family member will be shot. The information presented by each side seems to be on a different subject than the other. There is no clear clash of information that allows a listener to make a rational decision. In the debate about abortion rights, opponents of abortion present graphic depictions of "baby killing," while proponents of a woman's right to abortion show evidence that restrictions do not end abortion but only make it more dangerous and traumatic. In each case, further information will not change very many minds on either side.

As an example of ineffective information in a particular situation, suppose someone was looking for ways to persuade a friend to quit smoking cigarettes. Substantial information indicates that a nonsmoker will live a healthier and probably longer life than a nonsmoker. The smoker may argue that many personal habits and environmental factors contribute to diseases such as cancers and, if there are many other killing agents, kicking the habit will not necessarily prolong life. Second, when the friend presents information that shows the ill effects of smoking, the smoker may decide that the friend just happens not to like the smell of smoke and is only using the issue of the smoker's health when the real motive is a selfish desire for comfort. Finally, many smokers derive pleasure from smoking and may not want to hear or believe any of the studies or facts.

There is no easy way for the two friends to resolve the issue even if they are going to sit together and mutually seek facts that will be used to decide whether the smoker should quit. The nonsmoking advocate will discover information that tends to support his case, while the smoker will find examples of smokers who lived to be 90.

Information is important, but it is only one factor needed to persuade another party to make a change that the negotiator wants. People who overestimate the value of information might just keep looking for another study that shows ill effects of smoking, but an additional fact or study will probably not be what it takes to persuade someone to quit smoking. Even people who claim to seek objective information often have enough information. What they need is to know what the information means.

Exercise 3.3

List 10 important pieces of information that you have recently learned about diet and nutrition. If you were to give advice to a friend with poor eating habits, which pieces of information would you emphasize? Is there some missing bit of information that would help you give more credible or persuasive advice?

Information and its usefulness are often underestimated during negotiations. Sometimes finding just the right piece of information can help change a strategy or an outcome. The following are common ways that people underrate information:

- failing to search for appropriate information
- researching and planning prior to negotiation without accommodating new information as it becomes available
- focusing too much on the personalities rather than the issues
- relying on general information rather than finding specifics
- not recognizing the potential power of information with constituents or other influential parties outside the negotiations

Using the example about smoking, someone who underrated the importance of information might approach the situation without considering some information that could substantiate an argument by identifying and using only one study or example about smoking, by telling the friend that people who smoke have psychological problems, by emphasizing and reemphasizing the same antismoking facts or studies, by failing to recognize how information may have a useful but indirect impact on the attitude or behavior of the smoking friend, or by failing to see that information might have a strong effect on others who might be useful in helping to change the smoker's behavior.

The key to information in negotiations is not how much but what kind. Does it contribute to an understanding of the issues? Does it reinforce the case? Will it make an impact on the other side? Negotiators may need a quantity of information, but sometimes just one appropriate piece of information may be exactly what is needed. Negotiators can evaluate the usefulness of their information by determining its effect on the other side's perception or attitude. An employee may want a raise because the cost of living keeps going up, but, in arguing for a raise, she will have a stronger case if she comes armed with relevant wage comparisons or documentation of her exceptional performance. Some negotiators repeat information that makes a big impression on them hoping that it will also impress the other side. Usually they will find greater results if they repress their own tastes. The appropriate standard is to seek and use only that information that will have the desired impact on the other side.

Exercise 3.4

You are at a car dealership dickering about a new car. The sticker price is $15,000. You are willing to pay $12,000 for the car and have made that offer to the salesman, who has suggested that $12,700 is the best he can do. What new information could you offer that might change the salesman's last offer?

Using Information

Once a negotiator has found the information that is useful for supporting the case or persuading the other side, the way that information is used is very important. Reporting the findings of the Huthwaite group's research on manager's use of information, Hill (1979) maintained that successful managers use information in a positive and persuasive manner, as a basis for discussion and a reference point, "not as a club with which to bludgeon the opposition." He also reported that managers are more effective when they avoid using long lists of information to back a claim, choosing instead to cite only their strongest reason.

Interpretations of information are likely to vary greatly. So having information is not as important as the ability and preparation to make it plausible and convincing. The real negotiation skill is interpretation. Lying about information is considered unethical. Usually, it is a tactical blunder as well. Because most information can be verified, veteran negotiators will not get caught lying about the facts. There is, however, a great likelihood of distortion, exaggeration, and misrepresentation in the interpretation of the facts during negotiations. When faced with the other side's analysis of what something means, a negotiator will want to make a careful evaluation before agreeing.

Information can also be manipulated in the way it is pursued and disclosed. When each side seeks and protects its own information, the sides tend to become more competitive, but, if they are able to work together in a mutual search, both sides make greater gains (Pruitt & Lewis, 1975). In many cases, it is not possible or practical to work together in the discovery of information because of hostility, competitiveness, or fear of the other side. Even in these situations, when any single area of cooperation is found, the mutual search for information in that area can lead to the discovery of other avenues of possible cooperation.

In the decision to search, select, and disclose information, it is important to decide what kind is needed before starting. A small amount of relevant information is almost always more useful than a large amount that contains some relevant information. Overestimation of the importance of information creates extra problems for negotiators who cannot find exactly what they want or when the other side has valuable information of its own. Underestimation of information can lead to sloppy preparation and a reliance on general, ineffective, or irrelevant information. A healthy approach is to respect information, but not worship it. Negotiators should use their information wisely and sparingly with the knowledge that a joint search for information with the other side may produce more cooperation from them. They will gain better results using information as a place to begin the process of agreement rather than as a weapon for attack.

Using Questions More Effectively

Even as proposals are exchanged and debated, negotiators can continue to acquire more and better information to build their arguments by asking productive questions. Much of the movement that occurs during a session comes from the new information negotiators acquire in their questioning of each other.

Zemke (1980) analyzed the major purposes of questions in negotiations. He observed that questions are used to

- get information
- gain attention
- give information
- prod the other side to think about a particular issue
- bring about a conclusion

The most obvious purpose is to request information. If the other side knows something, a question may be the best way to find out what it is. Although it sounds like a simple process, respondents may not disclose the answer, or they may distort what they know. Who asks the question, and how the question is asked, may determine whether the answer is forthcoming and truthful. Individuals are likely to withhold or distort their responses when they distrust the questioner or feel that the information will be used against them.

The second purpose, arousing attention, is useful but overused in negotiations. When someone is not paying attention or does not seem to grasp the magnitude of the issue, a shocking question may recapture attention or make an impression. A problem with this technique is that its impact drops dramatically each time it is used.

The third purpose is using a question to transmit information. Questions can pass along information that would seem inappropriate or unacceptable if presented in a direct manner. Imagine the following utterance: "When I traveled to Paris on the Concorde last year, I found the food was cold and tasteless. Do you think that it has improved recently?" This world traveler is not seeking a review of the menu; rather, the question is posed as a method of disclosing that she is one of a very few elite in the world who have flown on the Concorde. The attempt backfires if the audience is sophisticated and unimpressed. Such a question may be noted as evidence that the questioner exhibits a strong need to impress others.

The fourth purpose is to focus the thoughts of the other side toward a point that the negotiator wants to dramatize. If members of the other side do not seem to follow the explanation, questions about what was just said—for example, "Did you understand that last point?" or "What do you think about my proposal?"—force them to think about the topic that needs emphasis. A major disadvantage of this technique is that, in a hostile environment, the response may have a more powerful effect than the question.

The final purpose is to close the deal or move the other side to agreement on a particular item. "Don't you think we can agree to . . . ?" or "If we have settled this matter, do you want to move on to the next item?" are examples of how a question might be used to bring a matter to an end. This use of questions is valuable, but, if it is used before the members of the other side have decided, they may be irritated and may even back away from the agreement.

Discovery of relevant information, presentation of a persuasive case, and completion of a satisfactory agreement are among the major negotiating tasks. Questions are tools that should be used to help reach those aims. Questions that impede or distort information received, those that hamper a negotiator's persuasiveness, and those that push the other side away from agreement are counterproductive.

A negotiator who strikes a tough pose or uses questions to intimidate may succeed in frightening members of the other side but may decrease the likelihood of getting accurate information from them. Negotiators who challenge the accuracy of the other side's response, who tell them that their answer is stupid, or who argue with their answer do not give the other side much incentive to tell the truth or to tell much at all. Sharing information is a cooperative process. Intimidating tactics and judgmental expressions deter the flow of accurate information. Even if negotiators do not like or agree with the answer, they should encourage the other side to speak freely; they should accept a response without judgment; and they should positively reinforce any behaviors that provide more or better information. .

Questions can reduce negotiators' credibility and thus curtail their persuasiveness. Simple-minded or patronizing questions make a negotiator look silly. Too many questions or repetition of one particular question also make the negotiator look foolish. Questions that reduce the level of discussion and questions that are asked for effect hurt more than they help. Intelligent questions are those that encourage the flow of information without hurting the negotiator's image. Questions that move the parties further away from agreement are not usually helpful.

Before asking a question designed to provoke a response other than the answer, the negotiator should think carefully about the hidden costs. If the question will drive a wedge between the sides, it may be better not to use it. Questions that are cute, hostile, biting, designed as put-downs, or designed to impress may move the sides further from agreement than move them closer.

Generally, those who want information will start with open-ended questions that allow the respondents to fill in the answer in their own words. Specific questions can follow for further details. In general, those who use specific questions first may miss information. They are more likely to look as if they are prying. After the other side starts to talk, then specific questions make the questioner merely seem interested. Without a very good reason, dramatic questions designed for effect should be avoided; they look good on televised courtrooms, but in negotiation they weaken the opportunity for agreement.

Questions are necessary to pursue areas of disagreement and hostility. Though the discussion may be painful, these areas should be discussed rather than avoided. Questioners who hear answers that seem inconsistent with the accepted theory or past wisdom should expand their ordinary questioning efforts to probe the inconsistencies rather than simply dismissing them.

Finally, while questioners do not like feeling that they are being deceived or manipulated, they should control their reactions. Strong emotional reactions to messages that are shocking or offensive provide incentives for the other side to lie, exaggerate, and use theatrics. To get accurate information and candid responses, the questioner must avoid quick or harsh judgments about the responses. Emotional evaluations of an answer provide momentary pleasure or relief, but they reduce the likelihood of obtaining more information. Productive questioners are able to show that they appreciate the candor, even when they do not like the response. To let the other side know they are interested and listening, negotiators withhold their opinion about the response as much as possible.

Information is one of the tools for productive negotiation. The skills at identifying, producing, and using information can provide the negotiator with useful benefits.

EXERCISE GUIDE

The moral of Jerry and Lisa's story at the beginning of the chapter: Jerry and Lisa each need a more precise picture of what they want. For them to begin a productive discussion, they each need more information. They need to know themselves and the kinds of activity that will transport them away from the everyday world and bring them back refreshed and ready to begin again. They also need to know about places, accommodations, transportation, and costs. In an adversarial circumstance, Jerry and Lisa each would want to compile the kinds of information that would support their individual goals. With a strong case for the "best" vacation, they could convince the other one or at least compromise from a strong position. In this case, however, they may enjoy a collaboration in gathering and sharing information and jointly planning the kind of vacation that will satisfy them both.

EXERCISE 3.1 If you are a union negotiator seeking a wage increase, you want to find the kind of information that justifies a wage increase. Specifically, you want evidence that the employer has the ability to pay and that the workers need or deserve the increase. Perhaps the cost of living has risen, or maybe comparable work is more highly rewarded by other employers.

Management will be seeking information that shows its labor costs are high either in comparison with its ability to pay or in comparison with other employers. Today, strikes are seen as the last resort for unions. The union negotiator would be reluctant to strike even if it seemed to be warranted. The negotiator would probably resist unless the members solidly backed it and it seemed that it would produce the desired effect.

EXERCISE 3.2 You will want more complete information about your individual preferences and about the available housing within a reasonable commuting distance. The decision to disclose or withhold information depends on whether you want to prevail in the decision or whether you want to make a joint decision. If the negotiation focuses too much on convenience versus tranquility, it may be headed for an impasse. Joint decision making might help find the qualities both sides want. In a complex decision, it is important to identify and examine all of the important factors.

EXERCISE 3.3 Some examples are fat, calories, sugar, carbohydrates, caffeine, alcohol, meat, sugar substitutes, infant formula, or pesticides. Do you and your friend share the same information about nutrition or are there some things that you know that could enlighten and alter your friend's behavior?

EXERCISE 3.4 If you are given an ultimatum, you may have to provide information that shows you could beat his offer at another dealership or an indication that you will be willing to forgo the purchase on those terms.

Making Cost-Benefit Decisions

The Story of Carla's Broken Windshield

Carla was driving in the middle lane of a three-lane stretch of interstate. Her speedometer indicated that she was doing the speed limit exactly, but she had to slow down because a concrete truck changed into her lane directly in front of her. As she decided whether to change into the far left lane and pass, a chunk of concrete dropped from the top of the truck and cracked her windshield. She honked but the driver did not respond. She followed him 3½ miles to his destination and told him that concrete from his truck had cracked her windshield. He said that he was not responsible, that perhaps a rock on the road had bounced up and caused the damage. She called the concrete company and received a similar response. Her insurance company gave her more bad news. She had a $200 deductible clause in her policy, which meant that she was responsible for the first $200 of a $300 replacement charge.

The insurance company did not offer much hope that she could succeed in a legal claim against the concrete company, but the agent suggested that she take her case directly to the concrete company and try to talk them into making a settlement with her. The agent advised her to write out her description of the incident, file a copy with the police, and take a copy to the concrete company. He told her that, along with her report, she should have proposals for redressing her problem. Finally, he told her that she may have a little leverage because the concrete company had been getting bad publicity about such incidents and clearly wanted to avoid a public issue, but, because she did not have any witnesses, the chance of gaining a settlement was remote. Carla does not have a lot of spare time, but she does not have a lot of money either. She believes that the concrete company should pay for her windshield, but she does not want to invest her time, effort, and resources in a wild-goose chase. Should she pay the bill and write it off as a bad experience? Should she ask them to pay the $300? Should she ask them to pay the $200 and offer to file a claim for the $100?

People who drive 15 miles to save a nickel on a loaf of bread do not save money unless they buy a lot of bread. The price tag on a product or service rarely includes all of the costs. Negotiation in a commercial situation may save money on a price, but, for an accurate picture, the costs of negotiation also must be calculated. Costs of achieving a goal through negotiation must be compared with costs of reaching it another way (DuToit, 1989; Lax & Sebenius, 1985). Expenditures necessary for constructing proposals, the time spent in negotiations, and often the costs of the setting, transportation, and communication should be included. Accessories that are not a part of the agreement but necessary to reach it should be considered. And, finally, intangible costs are always present. Negotiating may be the most mutually satisfying way of reaching a decision that affects more than one part of the costs, but it is not an inherently inexpensive way, at least in the short term.

Cost of Proposals

Analyzing circumstances, setting goals, and constructing proposals take time and money for research. Obviously, the greater the size and scope, the higher the preparation costs. Negotiating for someone other than oneself increases the costs of formulating proposals. Trying to discover what the constituents expect may be expensive. Polling, holding meetings, conducting elections, and using processes to build consensus always take time and usually money—a modest amount if the group is small, but much more with a large one.

The search for information to build proposals also may be expensive. For a parent arguing with a child about the appropriate bedtime, it may require a 10-minute discussion to determine that a proposal that the child go to bed at 9:00 on school nights is a reasonable one. For a company experiencing high absenteeism, comparing the pros and cons of the various absentee reduction plans may justify sending two managers to a conference and to visit other employers who have confronted a similar problem. It may require an attorney or an accountant, maybe both.

Preparing for a negotiated divorce settlement, the soon-to-be-ex-spouses reduce the overall amount available for splitting by hiring an attorney and perhaps a private investigator. But the discovery of some information about the sex life or character flaws of the other spouse builds bargaining power and has the potential for a high stakes payoff should the case reach the courtroom. In preparation for a presidential summit meeting with a foreign head of state, federal agencies, such as the State Department, the Central Intelligence Agency, the Department of the Treasury, and perhaps the Attorney General's office may spend millions of taxpayer dollars to brief the president.

Intangible costs constitute the third cost of proposals. Every proposal that favors one faction incurs political costs with another.

Costs of Accessories

Costs hardly ever end when the agreement is paid in full. Costs of implementing and adjusting to the new arrangement usually accrue. The cost of bread is misleading if buying it causes the buyer to pick up a jar of peanut butter and a jar of jelly. If that customer buys a new bread box or a new bread knife, some part of those costs may be attributed to the bread purchase.

The price of a new car is not the final cost if the new owner has to equip it with a CD player, buy a new garage, and pay higher insurance premiums. Clearly, a person adds to her assets when she builds a garage because some value of the garage should remain long after the current car wears out, but part of those construction costs belong to the car—the part that cannot be retrieved or used beyond the primary purchase. Whatever is spent because of the transaction, excluding its retrievable value beyond the transaction, should be calculated as cost.

Costs of Negotiating Time

Estimate the worth of the negotiator's time and multiply it by the amount of time spent in the process for an estimate of negotiating time costs. Protracted negotiations, especially those that involve large numbers of participants, can result in high expenses. Other costs should be analyzed at this point. If the negotiation situation requires that negotiators meet for a drink or a meal, the costs that exceed everyday expenses should figure as a part of the negotiation costs. Costs of a meeting room and related incidentals should be included. Even items such as laundry may be a cost factor if a starched white shirt is required on what is usually a day off.

Some negotiators rush their process to save time or incidental expenses. While it is always a matter of judgment about how much expense should be allowed to achieve a certain level of results, these negotiating costs should always be calculated and used to evaluate the effectiveness.

Exercise 4.1

Suppose you live in an apartment with a living room, kitchen, bedroom, and bathroom. You would like to buy a house that has a dining room, another bath, and an additional bedroom or two. You work 7 days a week for yourself in a booming business and have saved some money, but you feel that you lose money every hour that you are away from work. You are very particular in your tastes but have difficulty explaining them. You certainly do not want to spend a lot of time shopping around and haggling. You are planning to get married in 6 months to someone who seems to have no opinion other than "something small, easy to clean and maintain." Your parents are retired and have mentioned how much they look forward to you buying a large place so they can visit a few months each year. Your dad said he hopes you get a good-sized home so that everyone has plenty of room. You know that this transaction is going to cost more than the price of the house. But how much more? Design a checklist to help you estimate the overall costs.

Intangible Costs

Negotiation accrues some intangible costs beyond time and money. One's image and reputation are always at risk. It may be OK to gain the image of a nitpicker, but it is much worse to be labeled as devious or as a back stabber. The negotiation process puts both the mind and the body under tremendous stress, and the time spent negotiating may rob time from other activities, such as family, recreation, or health pursuits. A negotiator may reach a great agreement at great personal expense.

Exercise 4.2

A woman is scheduled to return to her family after a week away on a business trip. She called her husband last night and said she hoped to take him and the two kids out for a special night when she returns tonight. He is supposed to check with the kids and tell her the results so they can decide what to do. Daughter Mary Lou wants to eat a pizza and go to the last baseball game of the year for the city's triple A minor league team. Son Joey hates pizza; besides, he wants to eat at the fried chicken place that employs one of his girlfriends and then go to his high school's first football game of the season. After eating at home with the kids all week, dad wants everyone to go out to a nice restaurant and then something quiet such as a movie or a play. He knows his wife will be hurt if he cannot come up with something. Give him some options to consider, being sure to include the intangible costs of each option.

Figuring exact costs is impossible, but it is not difficult to make a reasonable estimate of overall costs. Research and formulation of proposals, direct costs of negotiating time, and how much the proposals will hurt or help personally and professionally should be added to whatever the agreement itself will cost.

Making Cost-Benefit Decisions

Effective negotiators will always strive to minimize costs by

- acknowledging all the costs of negotiation
- looking for ways to reduce the costs
- evaluating the costs in terms of the benefits derived
- not allowing cost concerns to weaken their bargaining position

There are many ways to save some of the costs of negotiating. For example, creating economies of scale is often a quick, simple, and lasting cost saver. That is, figure ways to cluster activities. Driving to the supermarket once a week instead of every day may save costs. Planning the research and scheduling of negotiating sessions can decrease costs.

Another way to reduce costs is to decide which resources are abundant and which are in short supply. If there is a lot of money, but only a little time, structure situations that require money rather than those requiring time. Reduce the personal costs of negotiating by being sensitive to the effect your actions have on the people around you. If your time will be spent in the negotiation situation instead of with your family, be sure that family members understand what you are doing and why you are doing it.

Most important, always judge the costs in terms of the benefit derived from the expenditure, not just in terms of the price. For example, suppose someone paid $55.00 for a pair of shoes worth $50.00. He spent $5 more than he should have but has exactly what he wants and $50.00 worth of shoes. While one who spent $25.00 on a pair that was not right will have shoes that sit in the closet or shoes that cause pain instead of pleasure each time they are worn. The first consumer is satisfied, but spent $5 too much. The second spent $25 too much and still needs shoes.

One problem that plagues overly aggressive negotiators is that, in their desire to take as much as they can and give as little as possible, they make deals that are counterproductive. Instead, they should give what they have to so as to get the level of satisfaction they need. Cutting corners is not always a bargain.

To make more effective cost-benefit decisions, negotiators should first examine their own priorities. One way to examine the decision-making process is determine if past behavior indicates that the negotiator is generally a risk taker or is risk averse. Risk takers are willing to take chances of losing what they have in return for the possibility of high rewards. Risk-averse persons are less willing to risk anything and more content to maintain whatever they already have. A risk taker will naturally choose the decision that offers the highest potential payoff, while the risk-averse person will choose the decision that offers the least potential loss. Knowing your propensities will enable you to moderate your decision-making behavior. Knowing the propensities of the other side offers opportunities for the negotiator to build acceptable proposals.

Another way to examine the decision-making process is to determine if one is generally an optimizer or a satisficer. An optimizer will continue searching for alternatives until a "best" one is found, while a satisficer will search until an adequate alternative is found. An optimizer may waste a great deal of time and money in the search process with the payoff of the best solution. The satisficer will save the time and money searching with the cost of a less than ideal solution. Again, recognizing one's own decision-making characteristics enables the negotiator to look at future decisions in these terms and perhaps alter decision-making behavior.

Cost-conscious negotiators can create difficulties for themselves if they appear to be cheap and overly concerned with price. They become easy to manipulate. That is, if the other side knows one's motivation exactly, often they can find a way to give whatever is requested even though it is not necessarily what is wanted. The secret to analyzing costs and benefits is simply to account for all of the costs and all of the benefits in securing an agreement and compare those estimates with the costs and benefits of alternatives.

EXERCISE GUIDE

The moral of Carla's story at the beginning of the chapter: Carla may have a very strong moral position, but she does not have a strong negotiating position. Unless she can find a witness or identify some other method of pressuring the company, she has little chance of reaching a fair settlement. If the concrete company offered to buy her a new windshield, they would be making themselves vulnerable to other claims that had less merit, so even bad publicity would not help Carla solve her problem. If

Carla examines the time, effort, and expense of trying to settle with the concrete company, she will probably decide to pay for the windshield herself.

EXERCISE 4.1 The cost of the negotiator's time may be substantial. Some negotiators spend hours before they enter into even a small transaction. Buying a house that will satisfy the needs of the negotiator, a future spouse, and other family members may require days of looking and researching. In this case, the expenditure of time may be justified because the purchase is so expensive and complicated. Negotiators who want to use their time efficiently will want to record the amount of time they spend on a transaction and evaluate that expenditure in terms of the size of the transaction, the likelihood that the transaction will occur, the value of the negotiator's time (at the time), and how much the negotiator enjoys or detests spending time examining options and reading the fine print.

EXERCISE 4.2 Identifying options that will satisfy the individual needs of a diverse group is often impossible. In this case, dad can satisfy his own interests, by ignoring the desires of the kids. He can choose Mary Lou's preferences or Joey's at the cost of hurting the other. The usual methods of resolving conflicts within a group are majority rule, alternating preferences, compromising on provisions, or ignoring particular interests. If dad wants to maintain an image of fairness and wants to create the kinds of experiences that will be appreciated by everyone, he needs to show a consideration for each person's preferences and propose a clear and acceptable method for addressing differences.

Building Credibility
to Enhance Your Power

The Case of the Summer Boss

Carlos has worked the past five summers at a small resort hotel and restaurant. This summer, Carlos was given the job of assistant manager. He enjoys the compensation, but he is surprised and uncomfortable with the unexpected resentment from the other workers. Most of them are older than he and about half of them work there throughout the year. They remember him as a high school student even though he has now graduated from college. He was given the job in part because, of all the workers, he is the only one who has a college degree. He has been accepted by a law school for the fall semester, but he still has not been accepted as a legitimate boss by his coworkers.

The nature of the work is such that individual workers can violate the standard policies as well as his directives, and he has little ability to monitor their individual actions. Work that needs to be done is not getting done and some of the workers' attitudes toward him are having a harmful effect on the customers.

Carlos has wondered about talking to the workers individually or as a group. He knows what he wants but he does not know what to do or say to gain their respect and to get them to comply with the work practices. What approach should he use? What should he tell them to gain their respect or at least their compliance?

Even in the most gentle types of negotiation, power plays a major role. Ury, Brett, and Goldberg (1988) suggest that a decision to cooperate or resist may depend on the key factors: interests, rights, and power. One side may reach a favorable agreement if it persuades the other that "our proposal is in your best interests." If one convinces the other that "you are violating our rights and our proposal corrects the injustice," both sides may move toward agreement. But interests and rights work best when the other side believes that failure to reach agreement may result in sanctions. Power, present in all negotiations, dominates the outcomes in many of them.

Negotiators' attitudes and actions affect their perception of the balance of power. Even though bargainers who use excessive force invite resentment and retaliation, power usually produces positive results for the side that possesses it (Zartman, 1985). Negotiators who are regarded as weak, especially if they also seem uncooperative and threatening, tend to provoke strong negative behavior from their more powerful counterpart (Michner, Vaske, Schleifer, Plazewski, & Chapman, 1975). Bargainers with little power make a major mistake when they force a confrontation with the other side. While negotiating is more than a struggle between two forces, each party still needs to possess some power. Each needs to know what power is and how to use it successfully. After determining what they want, and analyzing the situation to find what is needed to make negotiation possible, negotiators may want to turn their attention to bargaining power.

They need to ask:

- Do we have enough power to convince the other side to negotiate?
- Do we have enough power to achieve a desirable settlement?
- What can we do to build bargaining power?

Many enter into negotiation wishing or hoping that the other side will negotiate, but wishes and hopes are seldom enough. Is there sufficient strength to induce the other side to enter into agreement-seeking discussion? If there is, is it enough to get the proposals accepted? If not, what would? What are the components of bargaining power for the particular situation?

Too often, bargaining power is presented as the result of only one or two factors. For example, popular writers such as Molloy (1975) have given a great deal of attention to dressing in a manner that would increase power or "success." The proposition offered is that people generally do not know each other very well; what they really know is the image that others project. Because wardrobe and grooming contribute either positively or negatively to personal image, a change of clothes may significantly change someone's bargaining power. There is only a kernel of truth in that line of reasoning, because clothing is only a part of personal image and image is only a part of bargaining power. Such advice focuses on a narrow area at the expense of other important factors. It does not account for people who dress "wrong" and yet are successful. Some do indeed profit from enhancing their image, but negotiators will not want to invest all of their power-enhancing efforts into a new suit.

It is better to make a more general examination of bargaining power. What is it? Where does it come from? What can the negotiator translate into bargaining power? How does one estimate power? There are useful techniques for negotiators to use to identify and enhance their bargaining power.

Physical Power

The prehistoric ancestors of today's human race relied upon their strength to survive. Relics of ancient societies such as weapons, tools, cave paintings, and carvings show life as a physical struggle. Individuals were required to fight for food and protection from nature, but they also needed to protect themselves from each other. Those with greater physical size and strength had a clear advantage over the smaller and weaker. Ancient artifacts show the major role that physical prowess played in the patterns of human interaction. As societies proceeded to regulate physical force with formalized rules and laws, the physically powerful still kept their superior status. Twentieth-century humans inhabit a world remote from the cave dwellers, but physical size and strength still play a role in relationships. Someone seems dangerous when he or she appears to have the ability and inclination to overpower, contain, or injure others. Strong physical presence can be an advantage in negotiation.

Exercise 5.1

You have a 17-year-old son who is much bigger and stronger than you. He has declared that he is not going back to high school next fall for his senior year. He works about 15 hours each week at a nearby fast-food restaurant. He has enough money to maintain an old car and have some spending money but relies on you for food, shelter, and clothing. He is generally cooperative but becomes abusive when you say anything about school. What can you do?

The contemporary world is portrayed on television as a place where conflicts are more likely to be settled by threats, physical coercion, intimidation, and violence than by civilized process. In the real world, not all conflicts are settled by brute force, but physical power still remains part of the public consciousness. The reality as well as the cultural interpretation of physical power still influences today's interactions. When one person faces another in a dispute, the relative physical power of the participants forms a major part of the bargaining power equation. When two organizations confront each other, a similar type of power is displayed. Which is the biggest? The strongest? Will the larger one actually use physical power to accomplish its goals? Thinking of negotiating as a personal contest that occurs between two people clarifies the role of physical power as a part of bargaining power. At a basic level, each contestant has to consider physical attributes such as the size, shape, health, strength, and stamina of the opponent.

Exercise 5.2

Suppose we create a relationship between two people: If we make one a large, muscular, unshaven male, we will make the other a petite, frail, and sickly young woman. The physical images that they have of themselves and the other will contribute to bargaining power. Here, it seems that the male has the physical power to impose his will on the woman. If we learn that the woman is a martial arts expert, however, the woman's relative physical power increases. List some additional physical characteristics that we may learn about the woman or the man that might change the balance of power.

Physical power usually takes a more subtle role in everyday life. The evidence is clear that corporate executives and leaders in other organizations tend to be taller-than-average males. Do they have an advantage over others because as larger specimens they are accustomed to having their way, or do others generally defer to their larger size? Is size an advantage in organizational upward mobility because of some deeply rooted fear?

Social Power

Bargaining power does not consist of brute force alone. It takes place within a "society," and much of each side's power is derived from its standing or legitimacy within that "society." Some scholars see social power as orderly and civilized and therefore more appropriate in negotiation than the brute force of physical power (Boulding, 1977).

Exercise 5.3

Continuing with our case of the man and woman, suppose the relationship occurs at work. Because each workplace has its own rules and procedures that dictate rewards and punishments, the work setting is the relevant "society" in this example. If the woman is the man's boss, what impact does her position have on bargaining power? List additional social situations that would affect the balance of power.

Whether negotiations take place within the small "society" of family, work, school, voluntary organizations, or the United Nations, those who hold major positions, those who have achieved an honored status because of past deeds, or those who provide the group with a highly valued function have a place within that society that gives them certain kinds of power. The role of mother or father carries some authority within the family, but parental authority does not transfer to other kinds of social settings. "Teacher" may be a powerful role within the classroom but not so powerful within the school system. U.S. society reveres celebrities, the wealthy, and European nobility, while Japanese society seems to give more power to its elderly. Each society and each organization has its own formal and informal rules.

Exercise 5.4

Identify the sources of bargaining power that might be available to each side in negotiations between a 295-pound first-round-draft-pick linebacker from the state university and the 140-pound owner of a new NFL franchise. The owner is reputed to be the wealthiest team owner. The linebacker is known as the meanest kid in football.

Edward J. Lawler's study (1975) concludes that those perceived as having high status intimidate their opposition. High status bargainers are more powerful in face-to-face settings than when they use the phone, memos, or other indirect methods.

Technological Power

Bargaining power may be derived from the physical advantage or a social position that one side holds, or it may come from their usefulness or knowledge. Individuals or groups without strength or esteem find a source of power when they discover some ability or attribute that is needed or desired by the other side.

According to ancient Greek myths, their heroes enjoyed power as a result of their strength and attractiveness and power that came from an adoring country willing to grant athletes and warriors a godlike status, yet these heroes were no match for their wives. Upset that the men were absent from home for very long periods, one hero's wife, Lysistrata, organized a sex strike and curtailed the heroic travels. The strategy worked because wifely affection was deeply desired by these physically powerful, socially prominent men.

Workers with special skills, athletes with extraordinary talent, countries with precious resources often have a distinct type of bargaining power, but most people have a source of bargaining power if they can perform a service or provide a product that others value.

Exercise 5.5

Pursuing the earlier example, with the woman as the supervisor and the man as the subordinate: Suppose that the computer at this work location is vital to the everyday success of the enterprise, and this man is the only person in the world who can fix and maintain this irreplaceable machine. How does his skill shift the balance of power? List additional examples of talents or skills that either the man or the woman could possess that would influence the balance of power.

These three categories of power come from one's relationship with an environment. Someone in good shape physically and socially, with a certain amount of know-how, is generally in a strong position. In specific circumstances, however, polished manners may be preferable to big biceps and, when specialized knowledge is required, general knowledge or social status will not provide the necessary bargaining power.

In attempting to assess bargaining power with a particular person or group, negotiators should look for any resource that can be applied to the situation.

A negotiator can recognize that building blocks of bargaining power come from resources that will

1. pressure the other to move toward the negotiator's position,
2. serve as an object of value useful for trading, or
3. provide arguments and evidence useful for making a persuasive case.

In general, it is likely that the other side will make a positive move if they are appropriately pressured, if they are given something they want or need, or if they hear a compelling reason why they ought to comply. In assessing a particular situation, there are specific considerations that should be made.

Relative Strengths

As well as knowing the other side's positions, it is necessary to know their strengths and weaknesses. Negotiators need to know how much the other side needs them. What kinds of alternatives do they have? How long can they function without an agreement? How committed are they to their positions? Are they so strong as to be invincible? Are they so weak that they have nothing to lose in spite of additional force and threats? What do they want? How badly do they want it?

"How much do they need us?" and "How much do we need them?" are key questions for analyzing bargaining power. The more one side is needed, the greater their bargaining power. If one side is not needed or if its demands are too great, the other side may choose to end the relationship rather than bargain. High-wage workers in developed countries see their bargaining power erode in negotiations with multinational corporations because those corporations can rapidly and efficiently transfer entire work operations to a lower-wage domestic plant or to a plant in a low-wage underdeveloped country (Reban, 1977).

With this in mind, negotiators choose from several options: They may decide to keep their demands modest, hoping to show that the costs of the relationship are relatively low; they may want to increase their value to the other side to increase the need for their own side; they may want to find ways to eliminate or reduce the possibilities of competition from those who can make similar offers. Negotiators will usually want to look for alternatives to the current relationship. Choices give negotiators greater security and confidence.

Individuals who are totally dependent on another person (or think they are) have little bargaining power with that person (Bacharach & Lawler, 1981). Workers in a large factory that is the only major source of employment within 100 miles have little bargaining power unless they can create an alternate source of income or are willing to move. Nations that rely solely upon one other nation to provide a vital raw material or as an outlet to market their products have little bargaining power unless they have reliable alternatives available.

Bargaining power differs from other kinds of power in its basis in perceptions. Bargaining power is the amount of power that a negotiator thinks he has, plus what the other side thinks he has, minus what he thinks the other side has, minus what they think they have. In face-to-face negotiations, the personalities and characteristics of the bargainers influence the balance of power. They bring potential power to the table, but it becomes real as the negotiations begin. The personal power of the negotiators is a major factor because they must interpret and assess the power of the other side, and they are responsible for displaying their own side's power.

The leaders of the United States and the countries that composed the Soviet Union have great responsibility, procedural obstacles, worldwide visibility, and numerous constraints when they negotiate about whether they should each eliminate large numbers of their nuclear arms. In spite of the formal structure, their negotiations can be just as intensely personal as an attempt by two old friends to try to reach agreement about where they will meet for dinner. Even though many interests, job categories, work sites, local unions, and companies are represented in national labor-management contract negotiations, the personality and character of each side's representative will influence the outcome.

Bargaining power comes from the various environments of the bargainers and their standing within those environments. Negotiators will want to assess the other's relative strengths as well as their own within the physical, social, and technological environments. They will want to estimate how that power will be used during negotiations.

As they look for sources of pressure, for items with trading value, and for persuasive arguments, they will be examining the other side's needs, values, hopes, and fears, from the other side's perspective.

A strong tendency in negotiation is to try and figure out what the other side should want or should fear, but, again, negotiators are dealing with perceptions, and the key is to find what is important to them. What do they dream about? What are they afraid of? Negotiators who can find a way to identify the other side's needs accurately and can show them how a negotiated settlement can meet those needs will have discovered useful bargaining power.

Exercise 5.6

Divide into two teams. Each team should do the following:
(a) Choose a representative to arm wrestle the other team's

designee. (But do not wrestle.) (b) Assess the clothing worn by each member of your team. Choose the member you estimate to be the most expensively dressed and compare him or her with the other side's "clothing" representative. (c) Choose someone from your team who is able to describe how to change a tire on a Chevrolet pickup to someone who has never changed one before. After observing the comparative representatives (within each team), estimate how talented and powerful your team is in the relevant areas. Would a competition in these areas help or hurt you in future negotiations with the other team? How? In what kinds of negotiations? What cues do you use to determine the relative and relevant power? Are there steps you could take to increase your relative balance of power?

Building Credibility

On a personal level, credibility is the power to define reality and determine what is legitimate and reasonable. The negotiator's credibility is one of the most influential determinants of the outcome (McCroskey & Young, 1981). In simulated labor-management bargaining, management teams who believed the union's threats of strike were credible devoted more time to bargaining and argued more seriously about substantial matters than teams who knew that the union would not strike (Champlin & Bognanno, 1985).

In another example, Tedeschi, Schlenker, and Bonoma (1975) found that negotiators responded positively to threats from those on the other side who were judged to be high in esteem and attractiveness, but threats did not produce any positive movement from those judged to be low in esteem or attractiveness. In general, people are more likely to listen to and cooperate with people they like and admire.

In negotiations, the other side will tend to believe someone they find to be trustworthy, competent, and dynamic. Someone who can deliver on promises and threats, who knows the subject of the talks, who cares, and who is sincere or passionate about the subject is likely to be a credible negotiator. Thomas L. Friedman's (1984) studies of Middle East politics led him to the conclusion that extremists had more credibility than moderates because "they are ready to go all the way and use whatever amount of force is necessary to further their causes" (p. 50).

The first quality the other side seeks from the negotiator is trustworthiness. Those caught in lies or distortions will seriously damage their reputations. One who wants to be known as trustworthy should avoid dishonest dealings and seek opportunities to provide service. Making small commitments to people and keeping them builds credibility more than failing to follow through on large commitments or avoiding commitments altogether.

The second dimension used to judge negotiators' credibility is their perceived competence. When the other side judges the negotiator, a record of accomplishment helps while an image of ineffectiveness hurts. Showing signs of preparation, a grasp of the subject, and an ability to explain the subject in nontechnical terms help make negotiators look competent. Presenting a record of accomplishments for those who do not know them well, or building a record of accomplishments with those who do, helps negotiators to elevate their image of competence with the other side.

The third dimension used to judge credibility is the perceived dynamism of the negotiator. The other side wants to know whether the negotiator cares about the subject and an agreement. Dynamism is more believable when it is demonstrated rather than asserted. Jokes during a serious session, bored expressions, or signs of poor preparation all detract from the negotiator's dynamism. Certainly, a voice, face, or gesture can help demonstrate sincerity, but a record of experience with the subject and acts of concern are much more highly valued.

Negotiators who are considered important or attractive by the other side will be taken seriously. Credibility can be increased by demonstrating trustworthiness, competence, and sincerity. Regardless of the strategy they employ, negotiators will want to show that they are serious and firm (but not inflexible) in their dealings. Generally, they should avoid tests of strength: If they lose, they also lose credibility, but, even if they win, they are likely to generate resentment.

Building credibility is a matter of making and keeping commitments, threats, or promises. A threat that is not carried out destroys the impact of any future threat. Unfulfilled promises destroy credibility as well. If possible and appropriate, negotiators will want to make commitments just to show that they keep them. Once an offer or concession is made, it should never be withdrawn (Bartos, 1977). To do so violates one of the more fundamental unwritten codes. Negotiators need to be aware of their long-term credibility and be very careful about sacrificing it for some momentary gain.

Finally, in many negotiation situations, it may be impossible to be believed and trusted fully by the other side. Negotiations appear as a we/they type of structure, and that structure usually creates suspicion between the sides. Though the structural distrust is hard to overcome fully, the effort should be made. The more effectively the negotiators build their credibility, the greater the chances for a successful outcome.

EXERCISE GUIDE

The moral of the summer boss story at the beginning of the chapter: Carlos is confident of his technical abilities to perform his new job, but he does not feel that he has the respect he needs from the other workers. He could try to be "one of the boys," and try to win the camaraderie of the others, or he could take a tough stand and try to show them that he is boss. Neither approach seems appropriate in this case. Until Carlos has gained standing with the work group, he may want to deemphasize his role and focus on the work and the workers. At this point, he may find more success in dealing with the employees individually. He should use his superior education not to build a barrier between the workers and himself but as a resource to help identify and solve mutual problems.

EXERCISE 5.1 Power struggles do not occur on a single dimension. Parents exercise a moral, economic, and legal power relative to their children, but the parents lose their ability to physically restrain the kids as the kids grow. In this case, the parent still has the legal responsibility for the teenager but not much power to make him live according to her rules. Punishment might change the son, but only if the parent has the power to implement the punishment and withstand the resulting resentment. The parent may acquiesce to the son's demand, but the prospect of supporting a high school dropout is not desirable. The parent may want to focus the negotiations on the house rules as well as on the respective roles of parents and children, but the discussion should also include ways that both sides can help the other keep the agreement.

EXERCISE 5.2 The discussion should focus on how physical size and appearance influence the power balance between people. Size, maleness, roughness, and so on all contribute to our cultural interpretation of power. In this case, the martial arts expertise and the confidence that it provides should help to offset the power to some extent.

EXERCISE 5.3 If the woman has "boss" power, she may have the right to hire, fire, demote, promote, suspend, and assign work. This economic, social, and legal power forms the basis of workplace power. Even though physical harassment and bullying exist at work, management rights may create sanctions against them.

EXERCISE 5.4 The owner's economic power will be much more intimidating than the linebacker's physical power.

EXERCISE 5.5 The power to "get the job done" is a valuable type of power, especially when the skills needed to do the job are difficult to find and when the particular job needs to be done immediately.

EXERCISE 5.6 The ability to assess the amount and kinds of power and the ability to discern the propriety of each kind of available power are useful negotiating skills. While power displays may lower the expectations of the other side, they also indicate that the negotiations will be decided on the basis of power. Power displays that are polished and refined often produce perceptions of greater relative difference than displays that are crude or poorly prepared.

 Fitting Strategies to Your
Situation and Personal Style

The Story of Yolanda's Neighborhood

Yolanda lives in what might be called a transitional neighborhood. In her block, for example, the north side of the
street has charming, well-kept, 50-year-old homes. Across
the street are relatively new, nondescript apartment com-
plexes. The single family houses are almost all inhabited by
people in their fifties, sixties, and seventies. Most of them
have lived in their homes for years.

The apartments house students, other young singles, and
a few young married couples. Lights start to go out about
9:30 or 10:00 on the north side, just as the parties begin across
the street. The older residents complain about the noise, the
parking (they claim that they can hardly ever find parking
spaces in front of their own homes), the parties, late night
drunks, and the persistent rumors that illegal drugs are used
and perhaps sold in the apartment complex.

Yolanda at 27 is the youngest home owner on the block.
She gets along well with the home owners, and she has
friends who live in the apartments across the street (she even
attends some of the parties). Some of the other home owners
have asked her if she could talk to the tenants in the apartments. When she has tried, they suggest that she tell her
fellow northsiders to quit calling the landlord and the cops.
They agreed, however, to have her talk at the next renters
meeting. Yolanda is confident of her ability to talk to both
sides of the street but not quite sure how each side sees her.
She thinks that both sides of the street can work out some
agreement without any outside assistance, but she does not

know how to approach the apartment residents. Should she tell them that the problems have to stop or there will be major consequences, or should she try to understand their point of view and quietly seek to persuade them to change? Are there any other alternatives?

Though there are many ways to plan for negotiation, most everyday interactions do not include a thought-out strategy. Typically, a person starts from a problem, a want, or a perceived need: "I would really like to buy this." "I need you to help me." "I do not like this." Strategy often emerges while the transaction is in progress or as the participants fall into comfortable (though not necessarily productive) habits of accomplishing goals with others. Donohue (1978) found that the outcome of negotiations is strongly influenced by the initial expectations and by the implementation of a strategy. But what kind of strategy should be employed? On a practical level, negotiating strategy emerges from a consideration of the relative interests, rights, and power of the parties (Ury et al., 1988).

When people actually plan their approach to negotiating, they often rely upon advice or techniques that they learned from family, school, church, or mass culture. This chapter compares four familiar approaches or strategies that negotiators are likely to confront and to use. Each will be analyzed in terms of the costs, advantages, and propriety. These approaches can usually be categorized as one of the following:

- soft bargaining
- hard bargaining
- tit-for-tat bargaining
- principled bargaining

Instead of deciding which strategy to use, many negotiators simply react or rely on intuition, experience, or some social stereotype about the other side. As an example, Bartos (1977) found that, in general, women tend to take a tougher stand than men, but both sexes adopt tougher approaches than usual when confronting someone young, female, of another race, or anyone seen as poorly adjusted psychologically. In other words, intuitively, negotiators tend to take unusually tough stands when confronting someone who seems significantly different than themselves.

Or they may use an approach that satisfies their personality needs and fits their preferred self-image rather than one that is suited to accomplishing their negotiating goals (Spector, 1977). It is easy to adopt a particular negotiating approach as a result of personal characteristics, but it is more productive to think about each of them as strategies or approaches that anyone can learn and use as a method of reaching goals. Each of these strategies has a built-in kind of power; each leads to certain kinds of trades; and each generates its own kinds of arguments. It is possible to examine each one to compare its characteristics and its advantages and disadvantages.

Choosing a Strategy

Many people permanently adopt an approach with which they feel comfortable. They think of themselves as soft negotiators, hard negotiators, negotiators who are willing to give and take not only on issues but also to shape relationships, or people who negotiate from a set of principles. Each of these approaches provides strong advantages, but much of the effectiveness is lost if a negotiator falls into a predictable pattern. Ideally, one should be able to select and apply an approach when it is appropriate for a particular situation. Negotiators should use an approach rather than become one.

A soft approach minimizes or avoids the issue and the conflict. It works because many people respond positively to warmth and kindness; they are willing to reciprocate and appreciate your commitment to the relationship. Soft approaches are useful in everyday transactions where the stakes are low or in difficult situations where negotiators are able to call upon the importance of their relationship.

A hard approach minimizes the relationship and tries to narrow the issue. It works when facing those who have no formulated goals or plans as well as those who lack self-confidence. Weak or confused bargainers are more likely to comply with the proposals of a forceful personality. The hard approach is suited for short-term relationships where the other side is not fully prepared and is less likely to work well in long-term relationships or against well-prepared opposition.

A tit-for-tat approach does not necessarily give each side what it wants or needs, but it provides a basis for exchange and a sense of fairness. It works well when a relationship has endured past problems if both sides seek some improvement. It offers possibilities for one who desires an improved, positive, or normalized relationship with the other side but wants to move cautiously.

A principled approach proposes a method of respecting the relationship without suffocating the individuals. It focuses on the parties' broad interests and, as such, seeks to widen the scope of the talks. It makes its greatest claims for its path to win-win solutions. If both sides are able to suspend myopic, selfish interests and mutually undertake a search for creative options and long-term mutual benefits, it is useful. The principled approach's greatest usefulness is its defense against the force of personality bargaining. It offers great advantage for someone in a weak or minority position, someone interested in maintaining the status quo, and someone who is skilled using argument and evidence.

There is no perfect strategy. No approach works well in all situations. Because negotiators encounter various circumstances and people with their own sets of strategies, they need to be able to use an approach that offers what they need at a particular time.

Soft Bargaining Strategy

The central character in Arthur Miller's *Death of a Salesman* (1949) gave his sons some classic advice on soft bargaining: "Be liked and you will never want. You take me for instance, I never have to wait in line to see a buyer. 'Willy Loman is here!' That's all they have to know and I go right through" (p. 33).

The soft bargainer is one who attempts to prevail by being agreeable. Associated with chatty sales agents, with pandering politicians, and, in its extreme, with con artists, the idea behind this strategy is that others respond positively and generously to one who is nice. This strategy is widely used. One study of industrial salesmen (Spiro & Perreault, 1979) found that they were especially likely to use an ingratiating approach when they were confronted with "negotiating obstacles."

Others choose this strategy because they do not want to make waves. They attempt to be agreeable in all their dealings because they do not like conflict. Some pick a soft strategy if the issue is not important to them or when they are not willing to fight. Some feel personally uncomfortable with a more confrontational strategy. Others prefer a soft approach because they want to project an agreeable image. Parents of the baby boom generation relied on popular books such as Dale Carnegie's *How to Win Friends and Influence People* (1952) and Norman Vincent Peale's *The Power of Positive Thinking* (1952). The message was that being friendly and interested in others is not only a moral act, it also can be an instrument for gaining influence. Kindness could produce practical rewards in everyday relationships. Quick friendships could help make the sale or close the deal. These strong post-World War II prescriptions were reinforced by U.S. churches, schools, and television. They continue to influence the developed world as the emphasis changes from crafts and products to sales and services. The 1980s resurgence of boosterism and positivism supported an "if you can't say something nice don't say anything" approach to serious problems. Some viewed this revival as a cure for the cynicism of the late 1960s and 1970s.

During times when "agreeable" is fashionable, "critical" becomes the label for someone who is not a "team player." Proponents of this positive-thinking approach argue about the benefits of promotion and communication, while the opponents maintain that a "team-spirit" approach is a clearly repugnant publicity effort that masks and obstructs real solutions to the problems. Critics argue that much of the corporate and community efforts and resources that have been funneled into promotional or publicity efforts to win goodwill with the constituent or consumer could be used for better products and more competent services. Prospective customers are asked to buy not because of a preference for the product but because they like the corporation, store, or salesperson. Citizens are induced to vote not on the basis of issues or interests but because they receive patronizing reassurance that everything will be all right.

Though ingratiation, as a strategy for bargainers, has seemed more fashionable during some periods, it remains a durable approach. The spirit of Willy Loman and Dale Carnegie is present in the message of such "motivational" speakers as Zig Ziglar and

Robert Schuller. The message continues to be the same. The only major change is an adaptation to the more visually intense media of the 1980s and 1990s. The message now uses the setting and the props to build seductive, comfortable, and exploitable relationships.

Characteristics of Soft Bargaining

The soft bargainer is agreeable and flexible. Soft bargainers do not seek conflict; they do not want an unpleasant exchange. Even as they strive to create and preserve a positive relationship, they use the relationship to accomplish negotiating goals. Hoping to "attract more flies with a teaspoon of honey than with a barrel of vinegar," they employ this "strategy of nice" and anticipate reciprocity from others. They expect that a conciliatory attitude will produce a similar attitude in their negotiating counterpart. In situations without serious consequences, where the parties do not share much history, negotiators are often willing to "give about as much as they get" (Wall, 1985, p. 99).

Soft negotiators are not without effective tools. They can bring enormous pressure to bear in the form of guilt ("If you loved me as I love you, you would . . ."), sympathy ("It hurts me when you . . ."), implied threats to withdraw love or friendship ("I do not see how I can continue our relationship unless you . . ."), and other personal appeals ("You know how I am always there when you need me . . .").

Soft bargainers use their relationship with the other side as a basis for trading by making the relationship or the quality of it contingent upon the response to their proposal. The relationship will be saved or enhanced if the other side responds positively, and it will degenerate or end if the response is negative. Presents and tokens of affection are a bargaining tactic when the bearer of the gift expects something in return. Usually, they are willing to concede on the issues to reach an agreement and maintain the relationship.

A soft bargainer can make effective arguments. Using logic or emotion, they can remind the other side of the tradition of the relationship, evoke special nostalgic memories, or point out new possibilities for the future. Words and phrases such as *family, community, partnership, common purpose, mutual interest,* and *national purpose* are often used by soft bargainers proposing that the other side move away from private purposes toward some joint effort.

Advantages of Soft Bargaining

Generally, people reciprocate when someone is warm, kind, and agreeable. If they see someone willing to give a little, they may be encouraged to do the same.

1. A soft strategy often has enormous power for people who are lonesome or in search of a comfortable, predictable relationship. As life becomes more interdependent and impersonal, it produces a sense of alienation and powerlessness. It is not coincidental that business tries to effect a warm relationship with consumers. Except for those who see themselves as having substantial bargaining power in a strongly adversarial relationship, people are likely to reciprocate a concession for a concession (Wall, 1985).

2. Soft bargaining seems to elevate the relationship and, in a spirit of mutual self-sacrifice, it produces positive results without unduly harming the relationship. Parties engaged in a mutual soft strategy may find that both sides care about each other and as a result find a great deal of mutual benefit.

3. While many want to try a soft approach initially and use it until it fails to produce positive responses, soft bargaining may be more useful at an impasse. In deadlocks, soft bargainers consistently reach agreement more than other bargainers and, absent an adversarial relationship, soft bargainers produce higher payoffs for themselves as well as the other side (Leap & Oliva, 1981). When each side feels it has made more realistic proposals than the other, and when both sides have nearly complete information and a fairly accurate assessment of the other, one side may succeed in breaking the deadlock by softening its approach and demonstrating even further flexibility.

4. Soft bargaining is useful for those who confront individuals with a strong sense of self-importance. "High status" bargainers seem to feel insulted by proud opponents and are more compliant and agreeable toward counterparts who show deference (Tjosvold & Huston, 1978). In organizations with a hierarchical structure, superiors usually expect to be treated with some respect by subordinates. Even in more horizontally organized organizations, long-term members have difficulty accepting newcomers who

appear too aggressive. Some use a soft approach with strangers and a tougher stand in routine relationships, even though a soft approach has a greater payoff in everyday relationships. Soft approaches work well when both sides know each other well, when both face a common picture of the issues and alternatives, and when both share a situation and a vision that offers a mutual advantage.

Disadvantages of Soft Bargaining

Soft bargaining produces positive results, but it also has serious disadvantages.

1. In cases of representative bargaining, the soft approach does not give the negotiator strong credibility with the constituents. Barbara Reisman and Lance Compa (1985) argue that recent soft bargaining has cost labor leaders much of their credibility with the rank and file. They urge unions to abandon cooperative, concessionary postures and return to a strong adversarial stance: "American workers want an adversarial union, if they want a union at all. There is simply no other reason to have one" (p. 32).

Negotiators who represent others are at a disadvantage using a soft approach. Their constituents usually would prefer to see them as strong advocates. Creating a warm strong relationship may sometimes be the best strategy for reaching agreement with the other side, but for a representative it creates suspicion as it looks weak and ineffective to the constituents.

2. Soft bargaining does not hold up well against aggressive opponents. Hard bargainers may take advantage of a concessionary posture without leaving the negotiator an opportunity to recover. Negotiators who appear to acquiesce encourage the other side to increase their expectations and behave more aggressively (Fisher & Brown, 1988). In experimental conditions, bargainers who received large concessions from their opposition increased their own self confidence and adopted a much tougher posture than those who received smaller offers (Rubin & DiMatteo, 1972).

3. The soft approach often requires negotiators to give up more than they should because of the visible desire to preserve the relationship. Once the other side witnesses the commitment to the

relationship and a willingness to sacrifice to preserve it, they have an opening to become more demanding.

4. The soft strategy may erode long-term credibility because people will suspect that the relationship is maintained strictly for whatever can be exploited. As individuals and organizations build a "warm and friendly" atmosphere to exploit it for private gain, people are likely to become increasingly suspicious about the motives of soft bargainers.

Exercise 6.1

You work in a small factory that produces one product. You have learned that your factory will deemphasize the current product line in favor of two new items. There are rumors of plans to lay off some of the current workers, change job classification systems, and hire more engineers and computer technicians. You have no union and no legal standing, but, in the past when problems arose in your department, your co-workers always asked you to represent them. The word has leaked out of the office that the company plans to introduce some major changes. The workers in your department want you to talk to management. Many of them want you to suggest major wage concessions in hopes that management will not follow through with the layoff. What are the advantages and disadvantages of choosing the soft bargaining approach?

Hard Bargaining Strategy

He was as hard as nails and as mean as cat dirt when the going got tough. . . . He was a stern teacher who often tongue-lashed me for being too careless or too trusting. Whenever my inclination was to give the other person the benefit of the doubt, his position was that there was no such thing as the "benefit of the doubt" in business dealings. His approach was to tie the other guy's hands behind his back, bind his feet, close off all exits of escape and then "negotiate." (Ringer, 1973, p. 57)

In a popular paperback book, *Winning Through Intimidation* (1973), real estate salesman Robert J. Ringer shared his tough negotiating tactics as "secrets of success." Books such as Ringer's were especially popular during the mid-1970s. Hard bargaining became a popular image for a negotiator in business or politics.

In response to the social changes and the Vietnam War, cultural introspection flourished during the late 1960s in the United States. Public people were under new pressures to exhibit sensitivity and an understanding nature. Loud demands were made that institutions be democratized and organizations "horizontalized." Dissatisfaction was widespread. Advocates of change were disillusioned. They felt that no significant change had occurred and that radical transformation was still necessary. Established interests, however, were panicky. From their perspective, the changes had been rapid, radical, and usually against their interests. Powerful, autocratic leaders made phrases such as *hanging tough, playing hardball,* and *stonewalling* fashionable. The public model for the hard bargainer was visible. John Wayne and Bob Haldeman were succeeded by a wide range of tough-talking cultural "heroes" from Donald Trump and Frank Lorenzo to Hulk Hogan and Rambo. During the 1980s and into the 1990s, major U.S. corporations adopted a hard bargaining posture with their employees. Employers demanded large concessions and made "take it or leave it" offers.

Characteristics of Hard Bargaining

Hard bargainers appear tough and rigid. It seems as though it will be difficult to reach an agreement with them except on their terms. In adopting this strategy, they perceive, portray, and confront their counterparts as adversaries. They present a tough image because any sign of concession or compromise can be taken as a sure sign of weakness. Hard bargainers attempt to reach their goals through power, pressure, fear, and intimidation. Operating on the theory that people respond to threats and displays of power, the hard bargainer believes soft bargainers are naive and ill-suited to the "real world." The goal of the hard bargainer is that the tough posture will lower the aspirations of the other side. One hard bargainer may appear loud, aggressive, or overbearing, issuing "take it or leave it" orders. Another may have quiet mannerisms and imply threats rather than shouting them. Hard bargaining is not only a form, it is a refusal to make a conciliatory move or concession.

These bargainers use the force of their personalities to put pressure on the other side. The ultimatums they deliver are designed to make the other side feel as though they have no viable alternative to accepting the hard bargainer's proposals: "The only way that we can work together is if you . . .". Hard bargainers apply pressure by focusing on the supposed consequences of noncompliance: "If you do not buy it today, I can assure you the price will be much higher tomorrow." And hard bargainers use the power of their position to make the other side feel the pressure: "As long as you work for me, you will do it like I tell you."

Hard bargainers do not make trades except on their own terms. They want the other side to surrender, not offer to meet halfway. The trading offer that remains constant among hard bargainers is that compliance will be met with the removal or reduction of the threat ("If you want . . . , then you will have to . . ." or "Unless you want me to monitor you, then you must . . .").

Persuasion plays a crucial role in the negotiating ability of the hard bargainer. Those who choose this approach must convince the other side that they have the power to make the threat a reality, that they have the will to deliver the threat, and that the threat is something the other side wants to avoid. Tough bargainers may paint a vivid picture of severe punishment to be administered for noncompliance, or they may display their power or show examples of how they have exercised it in the past.

Advantages of Hard Bargaining

1. Power comes from the clarity of the bargainer's position and the knowledge that he or she will fight hard to accomplish the goal. Systematic studies of short-term bargaining show that "stronger" bargainers make greater gains than "weaker" bargainers (Dwyer, 1984).

2. The behavior associated with hard bargaining is effective when the source is credible. Sources who are perceived as having high esteem and high attractiveness produce more concessionary behavior from the other side than sources who seem to have less esteem and attractiveness (Tedeschi et al., 1975).

3. People often accept the proposals of a hard bargainer simply because they cannot think of a good alternative. Some are afraid and allow hard bargainers to prevail. Still others simply do not want to take the time and resources required to mount an effective confrontation. Sometimes, however, people actually prefer to deal with a hard bargainer. In an atmosphere of lies, deception, or suspicion, the hard bargainer looks straightforward and honest. And, finally, many just withdraw or surrender when faced with the hard bargainer's rigidity and tenacity: "If he wants it that badly, let him have it."

When both sides know each other well and have a fairly accurate picture of themselves, the other side, and the issues, hard bargaining does not work very well. Hard bargainers find their greatest advantage when the other side is confused or lacks information.

Disadvantages of Hard Bargaining

Hard bargainers may produce positive results, but with significant risks and costs.

1. They risk damaging their friendships. Hard bargainers are notoriously harmful to relationships. Their willingness to subordinate the relationship to their desires to be right and to win makes them poor candidates for good long-term relationships. Their aggressiveness wounds their friends and their inflexibility makes it difficult for enemies to drop their animosity.

2. They may meet someone tougher and more intimidating than they are. Hard bargainers may be a lot like the old wild West gunfighter: They win respect and compliance, but only until a younger faster gunslinger comes to town. If word gets around that someone thinks of himself as a hard bargainer, there may be a line of bargainers waiting to make their reputations by successfully confronting that negotiator.

3. They risk losing their credibility. Some hard bargainers begin to lose it quickly and some over time, but, because their claims and demands are great, they must prove themselves and hide weaknesses.

Once soft spots have been exposed in hard bargainers, they suffer an enormous loss of credibility (Wills, 1982).

4. They incur the high cost of enforcement. Those who bargain through threats of punishment must to be prepared to make good on the threat or lose all credibility. Administering punishment is costly. Hard bargainers must maintain force, monitor the use of force, and protect against retaliation (Schurr & Ozanne, 1985).

5. People try to bypass tough negotiators. Most will seek to negotiate with someone else or avoid negotiations altogether rather than confront someone who threatens and perhaps punishes them (Schurr & Ozanne, 1985).

6. Hard bargainers inevitably miss some good bargains. If they overestimate their own power, they do not have an easy route to back down and or to accept a less desirable settlement. By the very nature of their rigid posture, they relinquish the flexibility to reach out for available settlements that approximate but do not meet exactly what they proposed. Hard-liners may also miss bargains by spending too much time maintaining a tough image and too little time on substantial issues (Wills, 1982).

Exercise 6.2

One of your fellow union members has been suspended for 3 days for repeatedly parking in a space assigned to management. This is the first case of this type. The employee handbook states that employees are provided with free parking in the lot across the street from the office but prohibited from using the management parking lot. Neither the handbook nor the contract specifies any penalty for an infraction. As a job steward, you will face a supervisor who is known to be wishy-washy. You want a quick, positive resolution. The member who has been suspended wants you to make a very forceful demand to cancel the suspension. What would be the advantages and disadvantages of taking a hard bargaining approach?

Some negotiators express a preference to use a soft approach until the other side takes unfair advantage or fails to respond positively; then they will switch to a hard approach (Jandt & Gillette, 1985). In spite of its popularity, this progression of strategies is not without problems. Once the other side has determined that someone is a soft bargainer, he will have difficulty building a new image as a credible hard bargainer; the switch itself will cause a loss of credibility as well as resentment.

Tit-for-Tat Bargaining Strategy

> And he shall pay as the judges determine. If any harm follows, then you shall give life for life, eye for eye, tooth for tooth, hand for hand, foot for foot, burn for burn, wound for wound, stripe for stripe. (Exodus 21:22-23)

Throughout history, it has been said that human beings would make better choices in their actions toward others if they were certain that others would behave similarly in return. Reciprocal bargaining, commonly known as "tit-for-tat" bargaining, is based upon those assumptions. As a negotiating approach, it offers an alternative to the extremes of hard and soft bargaining and it proposes to make demands and concessions in an orderly, rational, equitable, and "scientific" way (Wall, 1977). If hard bargainers require "tough" personalities and soft bargainers are required to be convincingly "nice," tit-for-tat bargainers attempt to remove personality from the bargaining behavior and respond to others on the basis of "reciprocation." This strategy is cautious. It imposes a wait-and-see attitude. It takes small risks rather than large ones. Robert Axelrod (1984), a leading theorist and proponent of tit-for-tat, sees the strategy as one that promotes cooperation, even as it offers some protection against those not inclined to cooperate. Tit-for-tat bargaining theory is visible in programs, such as "assertiveness training," that promote goal-oriented behavior while rejecting both passive and aggressive measures.

Characteristics of Tit-for-Tat Bargaining

Tit-for-tat bargainers think of themselves as negotiators who motivate and educate the other side through punishment and reward. This strategy requires the bargainer to let the other side move first. When the other side makes a positive move, the bargainer responds with a positive move of equivalent value. When the other side makes a negative move, the bargainer responds with a negative move of equal value. By rewarding good behavior and punishing bad, the strategy is designed to reinforce the kind of behavior sought from the other side. Behavioristic in its approach, this strategy does not allow the bargainer to be fooled by kindness or blinded by anger and a desire for revenge. It is characterized by cool, deliberate, preplanned responses.

Those who use this strategy create a pressure or force on the other side through the pattern of their responses. Essentially, the other side is conditioned to make the "right" choice by the offer of cooperation and pressured away from a "wrong choice" by the promise of noncooperation. The power of the strategy comes from how much the rewards are desired and how much the threats are feared. The ability to articulate the exact behavior that is being rewarded and punished and the ability to remain consistent and persistent in the administration of the strategy are major factors in the failure or success of tit-for-tat.

Trades are the basis of tit-for-tat, but the trade does not necessarily involve barter over the substantial issues. If it did, the side who began with the most resources would have more to trade and therefore would dominate because at some point the other side would have nothing left. The nature of the trade often is simply behavior based on the attitude: "If you are reasonable, I will also be reasonable." The trades may be about the direction of movement: "If you give a little, I am sure that we will be able to give some also." Generally, what each side has to offer the other is its cooperation or its refusal to cooperate.

Persuasive arguments are a major factor in this approach. The arguments made are usually one of three types:

1. convincing the other side that the rewards will help them and the punishments will hurt them
2. convincing them that they will be punished and rewarded
3. providing them with a clear and comprehensive picture of when they will be punished and when they will be rewarded

Advantages of Tit-for-Tat Bargaining

1. In transactions, people usually appreciate someone's willingness to give them a sense of predictability, and many times they will be willing to cooperate.

2. When administered properly, the tit-for-tat approach shapes the behavior by positively reinforcing cooperative behavior and negatively reinforcing uncooperative moves (Wall, 1985).

3. Perhaps the major advantage to tit-for-tat is that it reduces the impact of the other side's personality in bargaining. A reciprocal bargainer responds in kind to the moves of the other side, making the other side responsible for its own behavior and the consequences of it. In other words, those who use this strategy will not be seduced by kind words or intimidated by tough talk, just prepared to respond, in kind, to the behaviors of the other side. When both parties have had past problems, reciprocal bargaining is an especially good strategy if both are unhappy with the past relationship and are prepared to move cautiously toward a more cooperative relationship.

Disadvantages of Tit-for-Tat Bargaining

1. Tit-for-tat bargainers relinquish much of their control as bargainers. This is because, in adopting the wait-and-see position, they always allow the other side to make its move first and only then do they respond.

2. Outright victory is impossible. Other strategies allow a negotiator to make significant gains over the other side, but in this one cooperative, equitable solutions are the highest goal one is able to achieve. While not always a serious disadvantage, the negotiator gives up the ability to get his own way and, with a disagreeable counterpart, the costs may exceed any possible gain (Fisher & Brown, 1988).

3. If the other side is shortsighted, hostile, or aiming for a win at any cost, it is likely that the negotiator will be involved in a series of punishing moves and retaliations without a viable escape route (Fisher & Brown, 1988).

4. It is difficult if not impossible to measure accurately the amount of positive or negative response that is appropriate for the other side's behavior. And, even when possible, it is difficult to make the disciplined response that is required. In general, people over-respond to a positive or a negative move (Axelrod, 1984).

5. The negotiator runs the risk of being seduced by the rhythm of cooperative moves while little or nothing is at stake and, suddenly, suffering an expensive loss when the stakes become high.

6. Tit-for-tat strategists may be perceived as manipulative—not in the same way as a soft bargainer but as one who uses the system or as one who is always trying to teach someone else a lesson.

Exercise 6.3

Let's return to the negotiations between the 295-pound first-round-draft-pick linebacker and the owner of a new NFL franchise. Write a scenario to describe how the owner might use the tit-for-tat strategy to negotiate a contract with the player.

Principled Bargaining Strategy

As a group they were unbeatable. They had been coached to play a certain way and they never deviated. They also never lost. What Bob did was to take you out of your own game. If he had a week to prepare for you, he would find a way to take away the things that you did best. (Feinstein, 1986, p. x)

Al McGuire's assessment of Bob Knight's 1976 Indiana University basketball team identifies a game strategy similar to a principled approach to negotiations. Bargaining theorists continue a search for approaches that can withstand the toughest or the most charming of the personality bargainers, approaches that can take the other side "out of their game." While soft bargaining is apt to preserve relationships, it is not as likely to provide a high level of accomplishment for the negotiator. A hard bargaining strategy might produce greater gains, but it also inflicts damage to relationships. Reciprocal bargaining costs are high, with its lack of control and difficult administration. What some bargainers seek is a set of principles, a game plan that they can learn to apply to succeed in negotiations. Theorists who attempted to construct such a strategy acted on the following observations and assumptions:

- People feel that they are disadvantaged and pressured into agreements that benefit the other side more than themselves.
- People who have achieved some success in negotiating see the personal costs that have accrued as a result of their methods.
- There are certain principles that promote successful negotiating outcomes while at the same time enhancing personal relationships.
- These principles can be taught and learned.

There are many books and articles, some of which have evolved into systems of seminars, computer simulations, and video- and audiocassettes. Among the more successful of these negotiating packages are the ones created by Gerard Nierenberg (1971). Many of these require specialized training, expensive kits, and a new vocabulary of technical words. Many use phrases such as *win-win bargaining*, implying that, if the plan is learned and followed, it guarantees profitable and agreeable solutions.

Getting Disputes Resolved: Designing Systems to Cut Conflict (Ury et al., 1988) emphasizes "interest based bargaining." In 1990, the U.S. Department of Labor developed and promoted its own version of "principled bargaining" known as PAST. It promotes interest based bargaining at its logical extreme (Barrett, 1990). The most popular of the recent negotiating handbooks is *Getting to Yes* by Fisher and Ury (1981).

Rather than giving a long list of detailed tactics and "appropriate" attitudes, Fisher and Ury's book presents a "game plan" that consists of four broad "principles." By adhering to these principles, a practitioner should be able to check the power of hard and soft bargainers, control the rhythm of the interaction, succeed on the issues, and still be respected as a nice person.

Characteristics of Principled Bargaining

To avoid the vulnerability of the soft bargainer and the reputation of the tough bargainer, and still remain impervious to the power of each, Fisher and Ury (1981) erect four "pillars" to support their "principled negotiation":

* Separate the people from the problem.
* Focus on interests, not on positions.
* Generate options for mutual gain.
* Use objective standards.

This approach emphasizes objectivity and the use of information. It suggests that adversaries are persuaded by solid argument, civility, facts, persistence, and standards.

There are several kinds of force and pressure available to the principled bargainer. Avoiding a confrontation of personalities will enable the principled negotiator to neutralize one of the main sources of opposition power. Avoiding positions and generating options pushes the other side toward commitment and certainty. The demand that the other side use objective standards reduces the impact of the other side's beliefs, attitudes, and opinions and may pressure them to argue from a weaker position. An opponent whose strength lies in the force of personal charm or conviction will be at a disadvantage because the principled bargainer asks him or her for facts, studies, records, and other data.

Principled bargaining reduces the impact of brute physical force and emotional power by moving the negotiations into a more mental and technological arena. Often, the side with the best ability to handle data and evidence will win. Principled bargainers also have a kind of moral pressure available. By demanding that only objective standards be used, negotiators assume the posture that they have nothing to hide, that they only seek the truth, and that they are willing to do whatever is right, once they have seen the facts. The negotiator appears to be on the side of truth and justice, often forcing the other side to appear contrary to virtue. Finally, the principled approach has great public relations power. Those who avoid emotionalism and rigidity appear to be more reasonable, especially when the other side appears greedy, vocal, or aggressive. In an age when images carry more weight than facts, a reasonable image creates strong, positive public relations. By rejecting the use of physical and emotional force, the principled approach defends against those who would use those weapons as it attacks with an intellectual, moral, and public relations force.

Principled negotiators search for agreements that move beyond the quid pro quo format because the highest goal is not compromise. The optimum in principled bargaining is not the situation where "I will make a sacrifice for you if you will make one for me" but one where "if we keep thinking and talking, we can find a solution that enriches both of our lives." By searching for creative options, the principled method works for enhanced trades, that is, relatively low cost for the giver and relatively high yield for the recipient. In distributive circumstances (my gain is your loss and vice versa), where enhanced trades are not available, then the principled approach is to seek a method that will provide an equitable distribution.

Persuasion plays an important role in the principled approach. Negotiators must persuade the other side that personality bargaining will not work and that there is a genuine effort under way to find creative options that will benefit both sides. The other side must be persuaded that, unless the principled structures are adopted, they will suffer from inability to reach agreement, intellectual and moral inferiority, or social and public relations setbacks. The basic line of argument runs something like this: "This is a new kind of bargaining where we put aside the old power-play tactics and spend our time searching for the methods that will allow us to survive and prosper together."

Because "principled strategists" work to impose outside objective standards on the negotiations, they put themselves in a position where they have to justify each of their demands. When they make strong demands of the other side, they need to be able to show that the demands are necessary, equitable, and beneficial (Abboush, 1987). The strategy works well if the adherent can draw the other side to adopt this method because it takes the other side away from their own approach and moves them toward the game plan of the principled negotiator.

Advantages of Principled Bargaining

1. Much of the advantage comes from the ability to diffuse the other side, to "take them out of their game," and to impose a new system on them.

2. A negotiator using this approach does not feel the need to rely on the strength or attractiveness of his or her personality.

3. Principled bargaining focuses on problem solving, discovery of mutual interests, mutual gain, and objectivity. When both sides have needs and interests that can be mutually satisfied, this approach provides an opportunity to make gains. It offers a format for finding a reasonable and beneficial solution to many problems.

4. Principled negotiating offers an excellent method for a weaker side to confront an opposition that has more power. This is because this approach uses methods that neutralize and avoid the other side's strength.

5. Principled negotiating achieves positive gains. This is because it recognizes the legitimacy of the other side and the effort is focused on achieving agreement rather than suppressing the other side.

Disadvantages of Principled Bargaining

1. There is a risk of searching for a common problem in the issues confronting both sides, when the problem may be in the person or people on the other side (McCarthy, 1985).

2. By refusing to take a position, principled negotiators often extend the negotiating time. Moreover, they may lose credibility and raise doubts about their sincerity when the other side cannot identify a specific stand. In many circumstances, avoiding positions is impossible. Those who are forced by their role or circumstance to take a position forfeit the ability to use a principled approach.

3. When both sides have strong and clearly conflicting needs and aims, with no viable options for mutual gain, they are forced to use personality bargaining (McCarthy, 1985).

4. It is difficult for one side to make creative gains or major progress using objective standards. Objective standards describe the status quo. They show what is, not what ought to be.

5. By rejecting personality bargaining in favor of principled bargaining, a negotiator may reduce the impact of the other side's personality and dehumanize them. After the bargaining has ended, if the negotiator needs their goodwill, enthusiasm, or creativity, he or she may find that it is not available to him or her.

Exercise 6.4

Your boss offered you a big promotion along with a small pay increase and told you to think it over and talk with her tomorrow morning. You want the job very much but feel that the pay should be at least 10% more than you were offered because of the increase in responsibility, headaches, and long hours that will come with the promotion. From your experience with your boss, you know she will expect you to be grateful and that she will not want to spend more than 5 or 10 minutes of her time in discussion with you. What approach will you take? Why?

Modifying Personality Factors

The negotiator's personality is an important variable in the process and outcome of negotiations. An understanding of the personalities on both sides should help a negotiator choose an appropriate strategy. As a simple example, people with a personal propensity toward risk taking behave significantly differently in negotiations than those with aversions toward risk (Barr, 1987). Risk takers consistently exhibit more competitiveness and make higher demands. Other personality traits are likely to help or hurt a negotiator. Those who can use personal strengths and at the same time eliminate, hide, or control personal weaknesses can be effective. Because of this, people are tempted to alter or disguise their personalities during negotiations.

To be a successful negotiator does not necessarily require a dramatic change of personality. In fact, a radical personality change might raise doubts about sincerity. Negotiators can remain true to personal values and beliefs without yielding to the need to inflict personal opinions and observations on others. Modest modifications of some personality characteristics are productive for those who have a clear idea about what they are like and what they want to be like. Personality factors can be a liability for negotiators who are unaware of their needs or their image. Those who are aware of their own counterproductive behaviors, but are unwilling to change, are also less successful than they could be.

To maintain a consistent level of success, a negotiator may want to explore the following questions:

1. Who am I?
2. How does my style seem to affect others?
3. How do I want to project myself to be more effective?

Self-discovery is a lifelong process. People may spend much time and money with psychologists or counselors and still feel that they do not really know who they are. It is possible to be effective without perfect self-knowledge, but negotiators who know their own strengths and vulnerabilities have an advantage. Those who do not feel well acquainted with themselves may start the process by answering the following questions:

1. What do I have now that I would not ever want to lose (my family, my home, my religious faith, my job, my inherited china or jewelry, my dog, and so on)?
2. What do I dream and/or fantasize about? What kinds of things would I like to do or have happen to me (win a multimillion-dollar lottery, find romance, become beautiful, help make my community better, star in a movie, and so on)?
3. What kinds of problems do I worry about (paying the bills, whether the kids are in trouble, an aging parent, things that need to get done, a failed relationship, a problem person, and so on)?
4. What can I do well (fix things, write letters, keep a neat home, talk with children, dance, sing, drive, find great bargains, and so on)?
5. What can I not do well (see the examples in question 4 above)?
6. What kinds of things make me very angry (racial slurs, people who tailgate my car with their bright lights on, the problem of homeless people, potholes, people who take advantage of me, and so on)?
7. What am I like compared with others (more ambitious, aggressive, active, competitive, and accomplishment oriented or more easygoing, laid-back, tolerant, and someone who just wants to enjoy life)?
8. Can I identify some of the major forces or events that have shaped my life and personality (strict parents, competition with a brother, a great teacher, a broken heart inflicted by a childhood sweetheart, illness, sports, and so on)?

Those who can list a substantial number of honest answers may not "know who they are," but they should have a guide for identifying strengths, weaknesses, motivations, propensities, and vulnerabilities. Thinking about oneself this way helps to defend against those who might take advantage by exploiting weaknesses, and it also identifies strengths that will help to achieve greater gains.

Some people understand themselves well but have a mistaken idea of their effect on others. Even though an individual's influence differs with the person, place, setting, and mood, close observation may identify some useful generalizations. A negotiator will want to notice and categorize the common kinds of behaviors that people exhibit when they are with him or her.

From a practical point of view, a negotiator wants to be treated as a good listener and yet wants to be seen as forceful and confident when presenting proposals. Those who seem to scare everyone away may take steps to keep opinions, advice, and complaints in check. Those who feel that they are rarely a significant part of discussions may find that they should employ some assertive measures.

Though people cannot control every aspect of their personalities and image, those who understand themselves and the effects of outside factors on their behavior can make some adjustments to increase their chance of success. Enough is known about how personality types react in general that negotiators can often predict the behavior of others and monitor their own. For example, aggressive action-oriented personalities (known as Type A personalities) tend to be more competitive than other types in negotiation even when the competition is counterproductive (Stensrud, 1985). Knowing that the opposing negotiator has a Type A personality will allow for the preparation of a strategy designed for a tough competitor. When a negotiator knows that he or a member of his team fits into the Type A personality profile, he will anticipate his own competitive instincts and take steps to keep them under control.

Negotiators who analyze their own personalities as well as those on the other side may find some insights that help in understanding the role that personal motivations play in bargaining. Spector (1977) found that negotiators often choose approaches that satisfy their personality needs rather than approaches well suited to accomplishing their goals. He found that cooperative bargainers need social approval; altruistic negotiators are moved by pity and wish to avoid conquest; bluffers and deceivers are motivated by needs for play, seduction, cleverness, and exhibitionism; and hostile bargainers are motivated by perceived hostility in the other side.

To develop a personality that works well, a negotiator does not need to become phony. Like other areas of self-improvement, individuals have some control over the type of personality that they want to develop or at least the one they want to expose in public situations. Characteristics that help a negotiator reach agreement or those that produce a more favorable agreement are the ones that should be adopted. This kind of self-driven, self-directed personality development is only possible for those with some self-understanding, those who can learn to see themselves as others do, and those who know what kinds of personal characteristics will help accomplish their goals.

EXERCISE GUIDE

The moral of Yolanda's story at the beginning of the chapter: Yolanda does not have the authority to solve the many neighborhood problems, but she does have the kinds of contacts that may allow her to bring together people from both sides of the street. If she can get representatives from both sides to acknowledge some common problems and to recognize each other as neighbors rather than natural adversaries, she will be creating an opportunity for both sides to improve relationships and solve mutual problems. Each side has some power to retaliate against the other, but Yolanda may help them to identify common interests and channel their power toward the problems rather than each other.

EXERCISE 6.1 The advantages of using a soft approach include the opportunity to display loyalty and team spirit. The assignment to act as a messenger with a cooperative offer is preferable to an assignment to deliver bad news. The disadvantages are that this concession is premature, unnecessary, and probably counterproductive. Without any reliable information about the situation or any knowledge that the concession will be reciprocated, this approach should be avoided. A preferred course would be to ask for information and offer a willingness to discuss the situation.

EXERCISE 6.2   In this case, there may be some strong advantages to objecting emphatically to this punishment as being ridiculously harsh and demanding that it be reduced immediately. Because you have no precedent, no strong contractual prescription, and a wishy-washy supervisor, an aggressive posture might give you quick results. The danger here is that the tough stand could create a hostile atmosphere and invite strong resistance.

EXERCISE 6.3   It is not in the owner's best interest to create a confrontation between himself and his prospective linebacker, but he does not want to appear to be a patsy either. A tit-for-tat strategy allows the owner to show generosity and an eagerness for a good relationship by building an agreement that rewards effort and results while it punishes poor performance.

EXERCISE 6.4   A principled approach should have some advantages here. With a boss who expects you to be grateful, you will want to refocus the negotiation away from the personal level and toward a professional level. Emphasize your ability to do the new job in a desirable manner and your interest in appropriate compensation. Because the boss does not favor long discussions, tell her immediately of your gratitude for the promotion but ask for a time that you can meet again to consider reasonable pay. You can avoid being unnecessarily demanding and still not commit to a job that does not give you enough pay. If you use this approach, think of options to increase your compensation. Possible options include more pay now, a pay raise in a month or 6 months, a performance bonus, a pay review in the near future, or some benefit, equipment, or perk that would be an agreeable substitute for more pay.

Choosing the Appropriate
Tactics

The Case of the Dean's International House

Twyckingham College is a small private institution known
for high academic standards. It has received international
publicity recently with its rating as one of the top liberal arts
colleges in the United States. Of the 600 students enrolled
each year, the percentage of international students has grown
from 1% to almost 6% in the last decade.

A benefactor is giving $5 million specifically to build an
international house on campus. The instructions are as follows:

> This gift shall be used: 1) to build and support the operation
> of a building and programs for the purposes of enhancing
> international understanding; and 2) to foster the interaction
> of students from all nations.

> With the guidance of the Dean of Students, a committee
> composed entirely of students shall design and monitor the
> operations of the facility. The members of this student com-
> mittee shall consist of at least 50% international students
> each year.

The dean is beginning to feel the demands. Shortly after
an article about the nature and the terms of the gift appeared
in the student newspaper, some of the art students formally
proposed a contest to design the new building. Some of the
international students think that the instructions are broad
enough to include scholarships for international students.
The dean has enjoyed many cordial relationships with individual international students but she has never met with

them as a group. Currently, the campus has students from 12 countries, each with different customs and traditions. The dean wants to include students from as many countries as possible, but she thinks that the ideal size of a committee should be no more than 7 or 8 total and that domestic students should also be a part of the operation to make this project a central part of campus life and to ensure that everyone becomes more knowledgeable and comfortable in an international environment. How should she proceed in the selection of, implementation of, and negotiation with this committee?

Many important contingencies of negotiation can and should be addressed during the preliminary preparation phase, but, even after negotiations begin, there may be lingering questions about how to proceed. There may be surprises that require adjustments to be made.

In one way or another, most tactics are selected to bring the negotiator toward a settlement, toward a victory, or both. Negotiators can discuss agreeable items early to build an agreeable atmosphere. They can offer the other side a limited choice to narrow the options and push toward a settlement.

Atkinson (1973) argues that, even in informal negotiations, an agenda should be used because it gives both sides time to discuss each issue in an orderly manner and it pushes them toward a final agreement on the entire package. The agenda should be followed closely enough to provide order and appropriate attention to each item, yet it should be flexible enough to provide some feeling of freed discussion and allow linkages on related items.

An agenda is useful for an orderly procedure, but the order and arrangement of topics can help or hurt chances for agreement. An important question is whether to start with the small issues and move toward the larger ones or confront the major issues first and then clean up less important problems. The first method is generally preferred. The advantage of starting with less significant issues and working toward the major issues is that both sides can develop mutual goodwill on the small items and hope that the cooperation will continue through discussions of the larger issues. Problems occur when one side exhausts most of its power trying for favorable agreements on the small issues and finding no ability to prevail on the big issues. Problems also may occur when one major issue is also the only real area of disagreement.

If, however, negotiators start with major issues first, and if they can agree, they should be able to handle the smaller items quickly and easily. If they fail, they are likely to continue to disagree as a matter of principle.

Exercise 7.1

Suppose that you are considering the purchase of a used clothes washer at a secondhand appliance store. You nod as the sales agent points out the features, brand, and appearance of each machine. You want a machine today and your major concerns are dependability and price. Nothing else matters much. You have heard that you can "negotiate" at this place. How do you order the topics that are on your mind?

The manner in which the items are grouped also may determine the outcome. Should proposals be considered individually or as a whole package? The answer to the question depends upon the nature and acceptability of the proposals. If each proposal is acceptable to the other side, it should stand alone, but, in circumstances where the proposals are generally attractive to the other side, with one or two objectionable proposals, the negotiator may ask them to accept or reject the proposals as a group.

The structure and style of negotiations also can have a bearing on the agreement. In many circumstances, there are no established guidelines for negotiating, while, in others, formal rules or procedures are imposed by tradition or regulation. Often, the parties create their own ground rules. Generally, weaker parties want change while stronger parties prefer to keep things as they are. Because formality usually supports the status quo, it acts as an additional hurdle for the weaker party and favors the stronger party (Morley & Stephenson, 1970).

Communication channels can be a factor in negotiations. Face-to-face negotiations offer advantages for those deeply committed to their cause because the visual interactions help to communicate the intensity and sincerity of the negotiator (Short, 1974).

Bluffing is a classic bargaining tactic. It is designed to trick the opposing negotiator by distorting reality and promoting illusion. Negotiators may feign weakness and/or pretend they have extra strength. In one common scenario, the bluffer will suggest that there is nothing more that he can do to reach agreement. His next step is "apparent withdrawal." Announcing that no progress seems possible and he is leaving the meeting, he secretly hopes that the negotiator will respond to the maneuver by offering a concession or some inducement for him to stay. These tactics succeed when negotiators swallow the bait and are pulled away from their own case toward the other side's. For a negotiator who suspects a bluff, often the wisest reaction is to wait in silence for the other side to come back (Hermone, 1974).

Patience will help negotiators avoid the pressure to abandon their game plan. Negotiators should not allow the other side to rush them, even when some of their tactics do not work as planned. Those who panic are susceptible to whatever the other side proposes. Negotiators may sometimes find it useful to remain silent for a few minutes to think at the table or to take a recess to refocus. There are few circumstances in which it is wise to make concessions because of fear, haste, or panic. It is seldom a good idea to capitulate to the other side's timetable.

Negotiators who are faced with powerful opponents often can avoid humiliation and defeat and maintain their dignity if they persuade and discuss but refuse to plead or beg. When confronting a person who takes an unreasonably hard approach, negotiators may want to find ways to defuse his or her power rather than increasing the tension and heat of confrontation. There are many ways to deflate the energy of the other side so as to foster positive movement toward agreement.

Standard defusion tactics include

1. giving the other side credit for ideas that you want adopted;
2. showing undeserved respect for the difficult individual— "high status" bargainers are more compliant and agreeable with counterparts who show deference, and they feel insulted by those who do not defer (Tjosvold & Huston, 1978);

3. avoiding the personality confrontation by acknowledging the other side's personal strengths while you focus your efforts on progress on the substance of the issue;
4. encouraging any unreasonable behavior exhibited by the other side—after collecting enough examples, use their behavior to discredit them with their constituents or with external parties;
5. offering showy but insubstantial concessions;
6. appealing to the personal interests or otherwise "buying off" the other side's negotiator in exchange for concessions of substance.

The negotiator who identifies a problem with the personality or personal motivations of someone on the other side must find a method of dealing with the difficult personality.

Exercise 7.2

There is always the possibility that one side wants to end the relationship: A husband wants to leave his wife, a customer wants to walk away from the salesman without making a purchase, or management wants to destroy a union. In each case, there may be strong pressure to maintain the relationship: The kids do not want daddy to leave, the salesman is an influential member of the customer's church and professional organizations, or management has a legal obligation to bargain in good faith with the union. Caught between a desire to leave and a duty to stay, the husband, the customer, or the management can push negotiations to impasse to have an excuse to do what would otherwise be difficult or impossible: walking away from the relationship. When the other side may want to terminate the relationship, which tactics would you adopt?

One of the biggest factors contributing to agreement is the negotiator's attitude toward the task. Those who try to control the other side are often surprised to learn the other side resents them. Those who count on the goodwill of the other side are often disappointed when goodwill does not materialize. Perhaps the most productive posture for negotiators to adopt is a hope, a desire, and a commitment to make the process work. Those who push for agreement look for opportunities to make an agreement a reality (Johnson, 1985).

Tactics for Negotiators Facing Pressure to Make Concessions

If the other side will not move and the negotiator must make a compromise to break the impasse, the original goals should not be abandoned. The negotiator may reassess the amount of progress that can be made but usually not the desired direction. There are specific traps to avoid. Inevitably, negotiators are confronted by someone attempting to apply a deadline to break an impasse: "I cannot promise that we can give you the same low price tomorrow." "Unless you agree to wage concessions by next week, we will have to close the plant and move operations to Guatemala." Negotiators will want to resist or avoid time pressures suggested by the other side. When the other side seems to be making a positive offer, negotiators will want to study it. There are very few once-in-a-lifetime deals available today that will not have terms just as good or better in the future.

When the other side seeks concessions, there is even greater reason to resist pressure for quick acceptance. Even those who know they eventually will be forced to make concessions should never be rushed into something that is not beneficial for their side. In ordinary circumstances, parties feel pressure to break an impasse and move toward agreement. But one should not act too quickly, because the other side may be under as much or even more pressure to move. Patience and the willingness to endure the discomfort of impasse often increase the pressure on the other side. One guideline is this: "Never make a Monday morning concession." It means, when talks resume after any break, a negotiator should allow the other side a chance to make the first move in case they are willing to make a concession to the negotiator.

As part of the deliberate approach, stalling can be a useful technique. Many times, impasses melt simply because one side loses patience or because they are unable to resist the pressures to reach a settlement any longer. As time passes and as negotiating sessions increase, particularly when there is some initial sense of urgency, negotiators reduce the level of their demands and their amount of bluffing (Pruitt & Drews, 1969). Stalling requires patience. It takes time, meetings, and pressure to help bring both sides to realistic expectations.

Those who have served as a representative in a labor-management negotiation often express surprise at how little progress seems to occur for so many sessions while sudden major moves are made at the deadline. Although this common practice does create some anxiety and some surprises in the rush to reach agreement, an early settlement is even more costly. It inevitably invites suspicion from the constituents about why that time was not used to make greater gains. Hill (1979) argues that negotiators should never allow themselves to be rushed, never give the appearance of being rushed, and take whatever time they need to accomplish their goals. This slow, deliberate approach increases the chances that the other side will come around, but in some circumstances it may mean forfeiting the chance to shape the configuration of the outcome directly.

Negotiators will want to determine if there is something they can get in return for the concessions. Conditional concessions are useful: "We may be able to move a little from our position on issue A if you will move on issue B." Negotiators will always want something in return for any concession. They should not give concessions that contribute to their own demise or continue to weaken their position. Onetime concessions are usually better than continuing or lingering changes. Negotiators should not negotiate away their future.

Sometimes the practical method of creating movement is to create a mechanism that postpones to the future the resolution of remaining problems or costs. A union negotiator has greater probability of gaining tough protective contract language or an extra week of vacation if he or she can defer the effective date for 3 years. A salesman has a powerful tool for breaking impasses if he or she has the authority to defer payment for 6 months or a year.

Even though negotiation is a rational act, the participants do not always act rationally or always make rational decisions during negotiations. Sometimes, members of the other side will fail to pursue the real interests of their side as they become diverted from the main purpose and focus on a less significant issue.

Exercise 7.3

If a potential customer for a new car has experienced frequent and costly automobile breakdowns in the past, a rational sales agent anticipates that the customer will seek a car known for its warranty, its reliability, and the predicted expense of repair when he shops for a new car. But what does the agent do if the customer is attracted to a car because it is red, even though it has a weak reliability record? An agent who wants the sale may emphasize the virtues of red. Others concerned more with a long-term relationship may try to point the customer toward a more reliable model. If you were the sales agent, what would you do?

Negotiators are usually much less successful when they try to help the other side get "what it should have" and more successful when they are able to deliver what the other side thinks it wants. They usually will find it more productive to understand the values of the other side rather than imposing their own values on the others. Negotiators who try to make decisions for both sides run the risk of alienating their counterparts.

When a concession is made, it should be given generously. The giver should make it special and never try to renege or moan about self-sacrifice. Negotiators who feel that they may have taken more than they wanted, needed, or expected from the other side should never apologize for their gains. At some point, they may want to consider giving some back voluntarily if they want to soften their power and increase their credibility through generous acts.

Exercise 7.4

Give examples of tactical errors by someone who abused his power or created unnecessary resentment. What costs did he incur?

The ingredients for successful negotiations consist of an accurate, comprehensive picture of reality and expectations, a commitment to reach an agreement, and a willingness to take the steps necessary for agreement. Anticipating what the members of the other side are likely to do, and empathizing with them, helps the negotiator to see the options that are viable to the other side. One who anticipates that distraction may be part of the other side's tactics will be prepared to pull the discussion back into focus if necessary.

Overcoming Distractions

A negotiator who has a very strong case and is confronting a skillful opposition should be prepared to face stalling and distracting tactics. The other side may try to bore, shock, anger, amuse, or confuse the negotiator. They may tell stories, propose committees, and outline numerous options in need of study, all in an effort to avoid confronting the case directly.

The two most common methods of distracting are changing the subject and handling the subject in a way that avoids discussion of the main issue.

Whether in simple interpersonal conversation or in complex and formal discussions, those who can avoid the issues at hand by changing the subject have a powerful tool to deflect the opposition from their goals. Negotiators may have to endure the evasive tactics of someone who asks irrelevant questions or injects amusing stories. The negotiator's response should be as follows: "That is very interesting, but the topic we are considering here is . . ."

The other tactic to distract negotiators is to discuss the issues in a way that focuses on the manner of discussion rather than the substance. Members of the other side may make their presentation dull, hoping that the negotiator will lose interest. They may use technical language or complicated information, hoping to break the negotiator's confidence or will. Failing to muster a strong rationale for their proposals, they may resort to personal attacks or more subtle slurs. Profanity or obscenity may be used if they think that the negotiator might be distracted by it.

The relationship between the two sides sometimes influences the effectiveness of distracting techniques. Christopher Lasch (1978) argues that an advantage of the adversary system is that it brings clarity to negotiations. The danger in overly cooperative relationships between negotiating sides is that they may forget who they are and what their interests are.

Before entering into any discussion or exchange with the other side, negotiators need to have a clear sense of their goals, because a strong sense of direction will make detection easier when the other side tries to be distracting. Listening skills are useful here because they help negotiators to see and understand the other side's main idea. Active listening helps negotiators keep up with the other side. Those who know that they are likely to confront distracting techniques will know what to listen for and be prepared to respond if they hear it.

Patience will help negotiators avoid being pulled away from their game plan. Those who panic become susceptible to whatever the other side proposes. It is unwise to make concessions or changes out of fear, haste, or panic. Negotiators should not allow themselves to be rushed, even when some of their tactics do not seem to work as planned. As a tactical matter, a negotiator's best response to distraction techniques may be to pause in silence (Hermone, 1974). If the negotiator cannot refocus the discussion, it may be useful to take a break from the talks and regroup.

When dealing with someone who seems to change positions erratically, the negotiator may want to insist that the person submit written proposals.

Anticipating what the other side is likely to do, and empathizing with them, helps the negotiator to figure out what options seem available to the other side from their point of view. One who knows that distraction may be part of the other side's tactics will be prepared to pull the discussion back into focus should those tactics emerge. Negotiators who understand themselves, are committed to their side, and have a clear understanding of their purpose have the essential ingredients for holding true to the course. Those who know their principles and stand by them are usually formidable.

EXERCISE GUIDE

The moral of the dean's international house story at the beginning of the chapter: The negotiation procedure is usually based on custom and precedent, but in this case the dean has few guidelines to follow. The procedure that she needs to create is one that will allow her to hear all of the relevant points of view, to encourage broad participation, to identify or construct the constraints, and to keep the expectations at a reasonable level. Initially, she should probably avoid meeting with any large groups who represent a single interest. By meeting with small, heterogeneous groups, she may be able to gather ideas and preferences without creating potential blocs of opposition. The dean should clearly outline and publicize the steps that she will take to develop this enterprise but avoid any specific commitments to outcomes. Her committee should include students from home and abroad but not separate voting blocs, if possible. The result of the committee's deliberation will almost certainly fall short of pleasing everyone, so she needs to make sure that the focus is on a procedure that allows everyone to voice an opinion.

EXERCISE 7.1 The question is this: Do you divulge a price range and then look at machines available at that level or do you appear uninterested in price until the end of the transaction? Generally, if you trust the other party, you would probably want to establish a price range first and determine what you could buy. If you do not trust the seller, you may want to wait until the end to discuss price, but, if the seller has given some concessions on delivery and warranty, you may not have much room to negotiate price.

EXERCISE 7.2 Pressure can force reluctant parties to negotiate, but often the negotiations break down when the pressure abates. The long-term strategy is to change the nature of the relationship and the focus of the discussion. The other side must be convinced of the relationship's value and the importance of agreeing on mutually beneficial issues.

EXERCISE 7.3 The sales agent can never afford to ignore the factors that motivate the customer. Identifying those factors and demonstrating their presence in the product are necessary. While the sales instinct is to narrow the issues and tailor them to customer demand, sales agents who are interested in long-term customer satisfaction should not be afraid of exercising their product knowledge and modifying the customer proposal or suggesting an alternative. But the sales agent generally should not try to impose personal values and tastes on the customer.

EXERCISE 7.4 Nations, organizations, and individuals who bully a weaker party pay a stiff price as the weaker party grows stronger. Negotiators who appear cheap, rude, or inconsiderate, and those who have slighted, wounded, or offended the other side, may also have a price to pay.

Organizing Constituents
for Representative Bargaining

The Case of Dennis,
the Discredited Bargainer

Dennis was never shy about expressing his opinion. Many of his coworkers would accept the workplace problems as a condition of employment, but Dennis would not. He made a point of telling his supervisor and demanding solutions. Fellow union members elected him steward in his department, which gave him official responsibility to take grievances and other problems to management. Dennis earned a reputation as a forceful advocate of the workers. Subsequently, he was elected union president and chairman of the union's contract negotiation team.

Dennis thoroughly prepared for negotiations and adopted a strong, aggressive posture in his quest for higher wages, better benefits, and improved working conditions. He expected the management team to present a strong and immediate response as they usually did. Instead, management only said that they would consider each of his proposals. As the bargaining meetings continued, management suggested that they were not prepared to make any substantial changes from the current agreement, but they did not confront Dennis directly.

They did, however, send a letter to each worker at home. The letter stated that the company was willing to make a reasonable settlement, but that the union bargaining team and especially "the team leader" were unreasonable. Dennis also found out that supervisors, even those who did not know him, were telling the workers that he was loud, rude, arrogant, and ineffective. They also spread the word that he had a number of unspecified personal problems and shortcomings.

Many of the union members are nervous because they hear that no progress is occurring at the talks. Some grumble that Dennis might not be the best person to represent them. At a union meeting, one of Dennis's detractors asked, "What are the procedures for replacing members of the union bargaining team?" Dennis has always been skillful at face-to-face confrontation, but he does not know how to handle this situation. What can he do to strengthen his position with his members? How should he deal with management at this point?

"He who represents himself has a fool for a client." That old proverb expresses the common wisdom that one is not always the best advocate for one's own cause. Until now, the concepts discussed in this book have applied either to principal parties negotiating on their own behalf or to bargaining agents. For someone who bargains as an agent on behalf of someone else, many of the guidelines remain the same, but there are some differences and additional considerations.

Principal parties see limits on their ability to represent themselves so they choose someone else to do it for them (Jones, 1989). They may need a lawyer, a sales agent, a purchasing agent, or a matchmaker. In deliberations between large groups of people, as in creating laws or constructing a labor-management contract, it is impractical or impossible for each individual to participate directly. Representatives are selected to negotiate on behalf of their constituents. The major considerations to be addressed in representative bargaining are the selection process, the role of the representative, and the authority of the representative. Political questions—such as these: "Who speaks for the constituents?" or "What are the duties and limits of the negotiator?"—add new and important dimensions to the negotiations.

Usually, negotiating agents are free to act more aggressively than the primary party. Representative bargaining assumes that the agent can function more effectively in that particular situation.

For example, an office manager who handles charges and billing procedures can enable dentists or physicians to allot more of their time to health matters. The doctor also can maintain an image as a healer rather than a money collector. The manager can negotiate the fees. In some situations, doctors who want a personal and professional relationship with their patients find themselves in an awkward situation. The personal relationship may make it difficult to confront or to prod the patients to pay what they owe because of a reluctance to appear pushy, greedy, or selfish with their friends. Without wanting to jeopardize a personal relationship, the doctor still wants to collect and wants not to feel exploited.

Agents often help to separate the personal from the professional. Through agents, principals can make requests that might be difficult to make directly.

The growth of trade unions from the late nineteenth century through much of the twentieth century graphically illustrates another kind of need for representative negotiation. Many workers felt a sense of loyalty and gratitude toward an employer, but they also felt that wages were too low, hours were too long, and job conditions were inadequate. As individuals, they felt helpless. Union representation offered a more effective means of confronting the employer. When workers simultaneously feel both gratitude toward and fear of their employer, it is difficult for them to pursue their own interests without their own organization.

Exercise 8.1

Recall and describe a commercial experience in which your personal relationship interfered with your ability or inclination to pursue what was rightfully yours even though you felt that you did not receive the proper service, product, or recognition.

Choosing an Insider or Outsider

When individuals or members of a group seek a representative, they probably look for someone they know and trust more than someone who has much more expertise. Negotiators who come from inside the group relate to the constituents differently than outsiders. Because they share the same experiences and outlook, they are more highly trusted. The constituents view the insider as having a better understanding of the group. Insiders display more confidence. They are more likely to have their agreements ratified and have their contract to represent the group renewed than outsiders (Klimoski & Breaugh, 1977). Insiders, however, lose some of their constituents' trust when they are strongly associated with one internal faction.

Choosing an outsider gives the parties a different set of advantages. Outsiders often bring an expertise that is not available within the group. They provide a more objective perspective, and they may help to unify a group that has serious internal divisions.

Choosing an Expert

Frequently, people seek a representative with particular skills and expertise in a field. Someone in conflict with the Internal Revenue Service might seek an experienced tax lawyer. A young man who has just been drafted to play professional basketball and hopes for a good contract will probably be wise to practice ball with his friends but choose a professional agent to negotiate his contract. Seasoned agents have greater expertise to confront the team owners. Veteran negotiators may be tough and demanding, but even the team owners are comfortable with them. Jan Volk, a manager for the Boston Celtics, expressed a preference for dealing with "competent agents" who have experience instead of novices. "Inexperienced agents and players," he says, "hurt the player by creating unreasonable expectations" (Bulkeley, 1985, p. 31). Expertise and experience are useful criteria for a principal to use in selecting agents. The agent should have the wisdom to reach a settlement and the resources to make it a good settlement.

Exercise 8.2

Both of the candidates running for president of your club know you well and consider you to be a friend. One is your next door neighbor. You like her very much and feel comfortable with her. The other is a vice president at the company where you work. You admire her and respect her intelligence and administrative style. Both have asked you to support them and play a leading role in their campaigns. Describe the decision-making process you would use in determining which one you would want to represent you.

Choosing an Objective Perspective

Ideally, agents should share the general ideology of the party (Jones, 1989), but the agent's main advantage is a better perspective than the principal's. For example, experienced job stewards should have an edge over the aggrieved workers in solving workplace disputes. Having handled a variety of cases, the steward should be more objective and better equipped to reach a fair settlement. The worker will be more likely to have a limited perspective and to take extreme action (give in too soon or hold out too long).

Bargaining agents seem able to assume a role and set aside much of their personal ideology during talks. Those without strong ideological convictions seem much more willing to compromise on major issues when they represent a group than when they represent their own interests (Rozzelle, 1971). Parties will want to pick agents with a stronger commitment to the ideology when they want to make a hard fight but agents with weaker convictions when they are anxious to reach a settlement.

Choosing a Representative to Reduce Ego Involvement

When disputes are serious, protracted, or personal, the positions and perceptions of the parties tend to become rigid. Often, they develop personal animosity toward each other. Agents often succeed because they have less of a personal stake and therefore less ego involvement in the issue than the primary person or group. Ego involvement is a crucial variable in negotiation. The lower it is, the easier it is to reach agreement, because lower ego involvement allows greater attitude change than high ego involvement. When the dispute is clouded by strong emotions and surrounded by parties who are more interested in winning than settling, an agent can increase the likelihood of an agreement.

The Formal Role of Negotiator

Even when an agent is used, the principal party still needs to understand the negotiator's job, its latitude and limits, and his or her expected performance. The role of negotiator representing a large group of diverse attitudes is a difficult one.

Those given leadership authority from the group will tend to agree with a position held by many within the group but not necessarily the typical position of the group. Generally, the greater the representative role and formal responsibility as a spokesperson for a group, the more cautious the agreement is likely to be. Lamm and Kogan (1970) found that, when they were asked to substitute, temporary replacement negotiators took much greater risks than the formal spokesperson. But formal leaders who are in contact with their group before and during negotiations are also more likely to take risks than those who do not have that clear-cut leadership mandate (Hermann & Kogan, 1968).

Structuring the Role of a Negotiator

The issue is not whether representatives are better negotiators than primary parties but whether a bargaining agent or team can do a better job in a particular situation. In fact, parties who look for a charismatic, talented agent with a terrific personality may not be choosing well. Klimoski (1972) discovered that groups tend to select better suited negotiators when they emphasize the structure of the representative's role and put less stress on the representative's personality.

Those who have a clear idea about what their constituents expect seem to outperform even the very skillful negotiators who are less certain of their constituents' needs. Still, they need flexibility to operate in their own way. In experimental conditions, negotiators with greater latitude to communicate reached more settlements than those who were censored by their constituents (Smith, 1969).

Negotiator flexibility seems to be positively associated with the ability to settle, but it appears to have less of an impact on the quality of settlement. Whether the group has evaluation procedures and punishment power over the negotiator or whether the negotiator has a free hand to reach agreement do not seem to be significant factors in determining the final settlement amount. In experimental conditions, both procedures seemed to work satisfactorily (Klimoski, 1972). In general, a clear assignment helps both the constituent and the negotiator, but, once the assignment is made, the negotiator needs room to maneuver to reach a timely and satisfactory settlement.

Exercise 8.3

Your 19-year-old son attends a university a few miles from a beach resort. He goes there with his friends at least one weekend each month. He reports spectacular bargains on renting condos and motel rooms during the slow fall season. The rates drop dramatically when people go in person to negotiate prices and accommodations. In October, your extended family agreed that it would be fun for all 14 to meet at that resort during the Thanksgiving holiday. Because you live closer than the others, they are counting on you to take care of the arrangements. But you do not have a free day until Thanksgiving. You could ask your son to make the reservations and negotiate the prices and rooms, but you have never asked him to do anything like this before. You doubt his judgment in selecting accommodations and you are fairly sure that he has never conducted any complex financial transactions before. You feel that he does not really know "the value of a dollar." But you do not know what else you can do. What kinds of instructions and latitude will you give him if he agrees to do it?

Individual Versus Team Negotiation

Parties who want someone else to represent them also may have to decide whether their interests will be better served by an individual negotiator or a team. Teams often can provide more political power and bring a greater diversity of skills and experience to the talks than an individual negotiating agent. Negotiating teams are valuable especially in situations as complex as labor-management contract talks or in other multi-issue agreement-seeking interactions between diverse organizations. Teams give constituents a greater sense of personal involvement. The experience of working together on a bargaining team preparing for negotiations provides valuable experience for the actual negotiating sessions. Teams that work well together exhibit a greater ability than individuals to work cooperatively with the other side (Schulz & Pruitt, 1978).

Among the other differences between teams and individuals are these: Teams tend to take stronger positions, issue more threats, and feel freer to deviate from norms or expectations than individuals (Dwyer, 1984). The style, formality, and range of topics discussed differ when teams are used rather than individuals. For instance, discussion in large groups seems more likely to produce more polarization in positions, wider latitude of statements, and greater attitude change in the opposite direction of propensity than when two people engage in discussion (Stephenson & Brotherton, 1975).

Individuals tend to be more conscious of personal feelings and less likely to make controversial statements when they interact with only one person. In a larger group, individuals seem more willing to be controversial or obstinate. With just a single agent for each side, the two have a greater chance of working out an agreement on a personal basis. An increase in the number of negotiators tends to make the proceedings more tense, formal, and suspicious. Individual negotiators can make on-the-spot decisions and can maintain a position longer, because they are free from the concern about a teammate's opinions. A team has its own advantages; they can spot the opposition's misstatements of fact more easily, they provide more balanced judgment, and they can more easily wear down the other side (Hermone, 1974).

Taking Advantage of Team Strengths

Perhaps the biggest advantage of using a team is that, in general, they represent the diversity within the group better than a single negotiator. In creating a team, standard wisdom suggests that the team should consist of different personalities with varied skills who are a broad representation of the group as a whole. That is good advice, but it does not go far enough. To be effective and credible with the constituents as well as with the other side, the group should be constructed to show unity in those areas in which the group is most likely to be divided. A team should be strongest in those areas where the group is thought to be most vulnerable.

In the construction of a team, negotiators should examine their own side for rifts or potential divisions that may be exploited by the other side. A group should look for differences within the group. Young versus old, male versus female, rural versus urban, rich versus poor, and skilled versus unskilled are some classic internal divisions. Divisions and cliques exist in organizations ranging from small work groups or churches to million-member organizations or large nations. Even when a negotiator has identified the splits (or potential splits) in the group, it still may not be possible to end the differences between the attitudes and needs of each faction. It is still very important that each constituent feels that he or she will be represented on the team. Negotiators will want each faction to know that its narrow success lies within the broader success of the whole group.

A group leader can resist being held hostage by the private interests of a powerful internal faction (a) by including members from the faction on the team and (b) by publicly and dramatically keeping the larger purpose of group welfare before the entire organization. A vague notion of unity is insufficient for team building; cementing the potential divisions is a crucial objective.

For example, if the other side finds some racial friction within a group, they may be able to exploit it for an advantage. It is not enough to respond by selecting members from each race for the team. Each person of each race in the organization must feel that he or she is represented on the team. Taking great care to avoid denigrating racial identity, stereotyping, or tokenism, the negotiator will want to work to promote individual identification with the purpose of the whole group. Another high priority is to look specifically for team members who can represent their constituents as well as make a strong personal and professional bond with teammates. Negotiating teams have the potential for delivering a message of great unity and strength if they are carefully and thoughtfully constructed.

Programming the Negotiator for Success

Negotiators who understand their roles, responsibilities, and the constituents' expectations deliver better results. The represented party can exercise a powerful stimulus when the party takes steps that build the confidence of their negotiators. Tjosvold (1977) found that spokespersons who were praised as highly effective by constituents were much tougher. They resisted compromises much more than those less highly praised regardless of the opposing negotiator's effectiveness. Constituents desiring a strong performance from their representative will want to provide a strong confidence-building pep talk for the negotiator before the sessions are to begin.

Exercise 8.4

A popular and powerful real estate developer plans to build a multistory tower for a nursing home in your neighborhood. While no one has voiced objections to a nursing home, the residents are very angry about the kind of building proposed. The zoning committee has scheduled a formal hearing to decide whether this project should be granted an exemption from the single family zoning code that is in place. While the zoning committee tends to favor almost any new construction, members of the committee have suggested that the developer meet with a representative or representatives of the neighborhood to see if some compromise can be reached. The executive board of the neighborhood association met and proposed three options: (a) Send the president of the neighborhood association to meet with the developer; (b) elect a committee of residents to go; or (c) hire an attorney that specializes in zoning cases for the meeting. List the likely advantages and disadvantages of each option.

Organizing Constituents

The Chicago Cubs' legendary trio, Tinker, Evers, and Chance, are famous for the record number of double plays they completed and are celebrated for their consistency through the early years of this century, but their spectacular feat is that they were able to create and maintain an outstanding level of achievement despite a deep personal dislike for each other. So intense were their feelings that, during one 3-year period, Tinker did not speak to Evers. Their superior performance came from an overriding concern for team welfare and a greater commitment to excellence than to personal feelings.

Tinker, Evers, and Chance were a rare exception. Usually, good interpersonal relations seem to offer a better chance of creating excellence in a group performance. In negotiations, organizations made up of members who feel concern for each other's welfare have a better chance of success than organizations plagued with internal ill will. Internal division, or a lack of identity or purpose, makes it difficult for a negotiating team to set clear and consistent goals. Lack of agreement within a group may be the single greatest factor in failure to reach productive agreements with others outside the group. When the division within the organization is apparent to the other side, negotiators operate under a serious disadvantage.

In team bargaining, the leader has alternatives for bringing a unified voice to the bargaining table. The simplistic way is for the team to follow its leader and provide support without question. While the leader may feel a sense of power to act without restraint, without the expressed will of the members, the team is not as powerful as it could be. A leader with a strong will and magnetic personality may be influential, but a leader with a precise mandate from the group has much greater power.

A second kind of approach is that the team may act independently of its leader and try to reach an internal consensus to impose on the leader. This process is more cumbersome. It does not allow for as much individual role comfort or efficiency as the follow-the-leader method, but it helps to create a more broadly constructed set of proposals. It also increases the likelihood of a strong active team in negotiation and strong team participation afterward in gaining approval from the constituents.

A third approach is for the team leader to seek prior approval for specific latitude from the team. This method increases the negotiator's flexibility though it limits his or her power. It should also increase the unity and power of the team.

Whichever approach is taken, negotiators need tangible signs that they speak for a powerful, united force. When they are the elected representative, their link with the constituents is apparent. When negotiators are selected because of their skill, experience, or expertise rather than their mandate, they may want active constituent participation prior to negotiations. Of the many ways of discovering the wishes of constituents, there are three common approaches:

- surveying opinion
- conducting an election for a majority mandate
- reaching consensus

Surveying constituent opinion is the easiest and most frequently used method. It may be in the form of polling, individual interviews, questionnaires, and requests for "input." This method yields a large amount of data quickly. In a large organization, this may be the only practical choice for determining member preference. Surveys do not, however, always uncover attitudes on sensitive issues or give constituents a feeling of participation. Often, questions are framed and administered to constituents, and participation is limited by the sensitivity and comprehension of those writing the questions. Polling and interviewing are weak because, while they tap private feelings, they do not predict how an individual will act as a member of the group. They do not account for interaction among group members, nor do they offer an opportunity for members to influence each other or their representatives.

Majority mandates include those methods that allow for voting and majority rule on issues or candidates. If a group chooses its representation through voting, there is some feeling that the group supports the policies and ideas of the one they choose over the ones they reject. Parliamentary procedure and referenda on issues allow for majority rule. They allow members of the minority an opportunity to vote, a chance to influence the group, and an opportunity to become a majority. But, even when these processes are executed with care and with justice in mind, those who lose the vote are likely to feel bitter and separate from the negotiations. In experimental conditions, groups who used an explicit agenda and a majority decision rule were more likely to form internal coalitions, block minority interests, and unequally distribute internal resources (Thompson, Mannix, & Bazerman, 1988).

When groups use a consensus-reaching approach, they achieve larger outcomes and are more likely to integrate group members' interests than groups who used majority rule. So, from the negotiator's point of view, it is wise to give each member more than a voice and a vote whenever possible. Ideally, in a divided group, one would want to make far-reaching efforts to offer a prominent opportunity to every member who wanted to reach the negotiators. At a minimum, some process for influencing negotiations should be made available to everyone. The group should learn that division and discussion are extremely valuable early in the process, but that internal criticism and debate are usually counterproductive when negotiations begin.

A thoughtful negotiator will want each group of constituents to feel that they had an opportunity to shape negotiations. The discussion between negotiator and constituents should produce a set of goals, a sense of purpose, and a sense of unity. Should internal tension make these elusive, the negotiator will want to examine the basic problems and find ways to ease the division. It should be easy to determine quickly whether the split is due to divided attitudes about the issues facing the group or due to individuals within the organization who are looking for status or political power. If the problem is with issues, compromises usually will be in order.

If the problem is trying to orchestrate strong independent personalities toward common goals and harmonious action, the challenge is to find ways of including those who want a stronger, more participatory role. Negotiators who need people to work with them should give credit and appreciation generously. A negotiator's primary purpose is not to heal the rifts in the group but to mend the fracture for strategic purposes; it is not necessary that everyone within the group love each other, only that they function smoothly. The job is to make sure that everyone can work together. The concept of "enemy" may not be productive at all in negotiations, but, if that concept exists, the bargaining power will be greater if members of the group think of the enemy as the other side rather than members of their own group.

The chances of unifying the constituents behind the negotiators' efforts increase when negotiators are able to involve the individuals in constructing the bargaining priorities if not the actual proposals. Those who are able to unify a group behind the goals of the team start in a strong position.

EXERCISE GUIDE

The moral of Dennis's story at the beginning of the chapter: Dennis's job is to build and demonstrate the strong backing of his membership, but, if he allows his personal style and characteristics to become the focus, he will assume an additional fight. He needs to remind his members of their goals and show that the management effort is simply an attempt to defeat the workers' effort. Trying to prove his "innocence" is nearly futile unless he can prove to those members that management has lied. He needs to use his interpersonal skills with his members first, so that his next confrontation with management is as strong as his past ones. Finally, he should resist complaints to management about their tactic because his complaints will likely be seen as indications that the tactic is effective.

EXERCISE 8.1   The discussion should focus on times that you felt someone took advantage of your friendship or kinship and put you in an awkward position. For many, friendship or the risk of losing it impedes good business behavior. Feelings of awe, respect, attraction may make it difficult to pursue a negotiating goal. In some cases, a bargaining agent is the necessary remedy.

EXERCISE 8.2   You are likely to alienate the candidate that you do not support or both persons if you decide not to support anyone. If your decision is based upon who you would want to hold office, do you want someone who will make you proud or someone who will grant you access? People often express preferences for candidates who win their admiration but actually support a candidate that is closer to them.

EXERCISE 8.3   If you choose to ask your son to make the arrangements, you will probably want to equip him with a set of guidelines that include the desirable qualities you seek, the price range, and the special needs that must be accommodated. Beyond that, it is desirable to provide him with a clear set of priorities. You may want to have him call home when he narrows the choices to two or three, but, at some point, you will have to trust his judgment.

EXERCISE 8.4 In general, an elected officer has the trust and mandate of the constituents but not necessarily the expertise. The president acting alone would have some flexibility, but the committee should be able to generate more options and provide the broader vision necessary for identifying problems. The committee should have the best chance of maintaining constituent upport throughout the negotiations, but private interests and relations among committee members might slow the process. The attorney should have the greatest amount of expertise in this case but will tend to be more expensive and less trusted if the settlement were controversial.

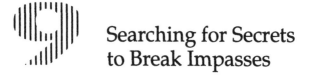 Searching for Secrets
to Break Impasses

The Story of Joni Jones and Her Parents

Joni was raised in a very strict home. She was not allowed to go on dates alone until she was 18. She remained at home during her freshman year of college, attending the local campus of the state university. She spent the next 2 years on the main campus, where she underwent a radical departure from her traditional upbringing. Joni described her life as "wild" and admits to making up for lost time, but, in spite of exercising her new freedom, she remained a straight A student. Joni tried to mask her new life when she saw her parents, but, on a visit home at the end of her junior year, she found herself in a terrible argument with her parents. She accused them of being out of touch with the real world. They condemned her life-style. They also told her that their support for her life-style was finished. They would pay for the rest of her schooling only if she were to drop out at the main campus, move back home, conform to their life-style, and finish her degree at the local campus. All of the terms are unacceptable to her. She likes her life. She is an adult and anyway it would take 2 years more for her to get the needed courses at the local campus. What really enrages her is that her grandfather (now dead) gave her parents the money to send each of the kids through school. Her parents supported her two older brothers through law school and medical school, respectively. She knows that her parents never judged her brothers by their life-styles as long as they maintained good grades. Her life-style is not any "worse" than theirs and her grades are considerably better. She loves her parents but does not want to live as they do. They told her that, if she goes out on her own, she should not come back. Neither side seems willing to budge. Do you have any advice for Joni?

Of the major negotiating problems, one of the most puzzling is how to break an impasse. Obviously, some conflicts are difficult to settle, but the cases that are hard to understand are those in which agreement proves elusive despite obviously available solutions. Margaret A. Neale and Max H. Bazerman (1985a, p. 34) surveyed previous research looking for the answer to the question: "How can so many negotiators with clear possibilities and common ground necessary for agreement, and with strong pressure to settle, still find themselves unable to reach an understanding?" They found three common patterns that are often associated with impasses:

- The basic proposals were agreeable, but one factor (political position or personality conflict) made settlement seem out of reach.
- Issues and proposals were acceptable, but they were framed in a way that made them difficult to accept.
- Negotiators were overconfident or held excessive expectations, making it difficult for them to reevaluate or seek a realistic goal.

Exercise 9.1

Identify an impasse that currently exists between two countries, between a business and consumers, and between two individuals. In each of these cases, outline the circumstances of the stalemate. Do the scenarios fit into one of these common patterns?

Even those negotiations with all the ingredients thought necessary to provide successful outcomes for both parties have the potential of breaking down. Some negotiators become angry when they reach an impasse, some become stubborn, and others panic. These behaviors are unlikely to bring about a quick solution.

Perhaps the worst response to an impasse, however, is to make a major concession in fear or in hope that the other side will also make a large move toward the negotiator. When negotiators make a big concession, they invite the other side to take an even harder stance. Big concessions are an admission that the negotiator had been asking for too much. A large concession justifies the position of the other side (Yukl, 1974). Other possibilities may be difficult, but they are more desirable if negotiators prefer to see the other side eventually make substantial conciliatory moves.

Strategies for Producing Movement in the Other Side

What causes one of the parties to move in the other's direction? Abboush (1987) examined union behavior when faced with a management demand for concessions. His conclusions were consistent with Neale and Bazerman's (1985a) findings. He identified three conditions responsible for increasing the likelihood that a union would try to end an impasse by granting concessions: pressure externally imposed on the union; reduced militancy, which he describes as an internal state of the union; and discovery of new legitimacy for the concessions demanded. Abboush's findings may be generalized to fit other situations. A negotiator can break an impasse and promote movement from the other side by

1. increasing application of his or her bargaining strength,
2. reducing the bargaining strength of the other side, or
3. introducing new circumstances, new proposals, new solutions, new justifications, new information, or new perspectives into the talks.

The first strategy is to use or increase force to make the other side move. A show of strength or other pressure may be used to create doubts and lower expectations on the other side. If that pressure is credible and is seen as a sign of the negotiator's resolve, it may bring about a positive move from the other side.

The second strategy is designed to weaken the resolve or power of the other side. Specific tactics that can be used are to stall, to discredit individuals on the other side, to agree in principle without agreeing to any specific proposal, to grant some concessions, or to reduce the animosity (remove the other side's reason to hate the negotiator or to use him or her as a symbol of oppression or injustice). These approaches require a search for the other side's underlying strength as well as an effort to eliminate or undermine it.

The third strategy requires negotiators to introduce new circumstances, new proposals, new solutions, new information, or new perspectives into the negotiations. The negotiator tries to remove the obstacles to settlement by finding a way around them or by moving them to the side, to the past, or to the future. Some experts suggest using a "side bar," which is essentially reconvening in a less formal setting in an attempt to find some movement in the deadlock (Kasprzak, 1986).

Negotiators who are caught in an impasse and not inclined to make concessions will want to choose an impasse-breaking strategy in terms of the specific circumstances, determining which one is appropriate in each case. By considering the following examples, it is possible to see the advantages and disadvantages of each strategy.

Exercise 9.2

When both sides have numerous questions and similar kinds of doubts, the result is often impasse. Both sides take a rigid position and wait for the other side to make the first concession. As a result, there is no progress. Which strategy would you adopt?

In this first example, both sides are unsure of themselves and their opposition. The use or the increase of pressure or force may produce desired results. The demonstration of strength may reduce the aspirations and will of the other side. If they have doubts and those doubts are exploited, they will probably offer a compromise. If the show of strength is not credible and formidable, however, members of the other side may actually enjoy an increase in confidence. They may refuse to compromise or even escalate demands. Where members of both sides lack information and doubt themselves, negotiators who can reduce the confidence or create more doubts on the other side may gain an advantage and promote movement. The danger of this strategy is that, if the other side becomes suspicious, they may seek outside information, resist, or end the negotiations.

The third strategy is generally not the preferred choice when there is doubt and confusion on the other side. New terms may only leave members of the other side more confused and doubtful. For them to move, they would need strong, clear, forceful leadership, not several new choices. But this strategy is useful when some concrete objection is identified and isolated. The negotiator can often create movement by introducing one specific new proposal.

Exercise 9.3

Consider another set of circumstances in which both sides have a fairly accurate view of the situation, themselves, and their counterpart, but, because they both want something that the other does not want to give, they too are at impasse. Which strategy would you adopt?

In this second example, both sides have relatively complete information, but neither wants to bear the costs of conceding. Here, increased pressure may have little power to produce movement unless the pressure comes from an unexpected source or with unexpected force. Because both sides know each other and have a predictable relationship, breaking an impasse may require a significant amount of force to move the other side. Sometimes a threat from a source outside the negotiations will provide a sufficient push to restart the talks.

When both sides have an accurate grasp of the situation, attempts to weaken or undermine the other side will be a difficult strategy to employ. The other side is likely to have realistic self-confidence that provides them a sense of strength. The introduction of something new may be the right prescription when the stuck parties both have fairly accurate information. A substantial change may be necessary to break the impasse, but it may take only a change of focus or a new talking point to help both sides find new hope for mutual progress. In this situation, it is not unreasonable for the negotiator to make a small concession or move toward the other side. With complete information available,

the other side should be able to recognize the value of the negotiator's move and not mistake it for weakness.

Exercise 9.4

**A common example of circumstances that lead to impasse is
one side taking an unwarranted tough stand. Sometimes because of constituent pressure, sometimes because a personal
reputation is at stake, and sometimes because of an unrealistic
self-image or some strong personal motive, the negotiator for
one side will push the discussion to impasse. Which strategy
would you adopt to counter the impasse?**

In this example, the other side is led by a person with a massive
ego, a tough posture, a need for revenge, or a constituency that is
demanding. Pressure can be used if it is strong and focused enough
to discourage the other side thoroughly. Insufficient pressure will
only serve as a challenge for the other side to counter with whatever weapons it possesses.

The strategy of introducing new terms or perspectives is not
likely to be effective unless the terms are seen as a concession.
When some factor other than the issues on the table is creating the
impasse, changing those issues, or the perceptions of those issues,
will not help.

In this last example, one side may have manufactured the break-
down in the talks and used it as an excuse to end the relationship;
maybe it wants out of the relationship. If so, force or pressure may
help promote movement, but the negotiator should expect resistance. Many times, the application of pressure will only increase
the desire to terminate the relationship.

Those who create or use an impasse to end a relationship may
not respond positively to negotiators who try to weaken or discredit them. If the aim is to destroy or desert the negotiations,
discrediting will help only if a sense of shame, remorse, or impo-
tence will make them discover how much they need an agreement
and how much worse their existence will be alone. Efforts to
undermine will likely engender more bitterness and resentment
and provide further justification to break the relationship. Where
the impasse is created to offer a cover for breaking the relationship,

redefining the terms of the relationship is the strategy offering the most hope. Unless the other side can be made to see new issues, new advantages, new relationship terms, and new reasons for continuing, pressure and undermining attempts will provide slim chances for positive movement.

Some negotiators find themselves at an impasse even though they are able to resolve the major issues. They fail to reach agreement because of a minor dispute. A negotiator's job is to make it easy for the other side to reach agreement once the major issues have been settled. By identifying and overcoming the minor hitches, the negotiator will have discovered a real secret to creating movement. Sometimes it is necessary to redefine the issues or to create detailed guidelines, extraordinary assurances, or elaborate financial plans to conclude a transaction (Galowitz, 1979).

The solution to breaking an impasse by inducing the other side to move lies within three general guidelines:

- increasing the pressure on the other side
- reducing their strength and ability to bring pressure
- changing the nature of the issue by introducing something new into the talks

Negotiators should not be afraid of impasse. They can profitably use it to clarify their own goals and their fundamental disagreement with the other side and build creative solutions to their problems (Druckman, 1986).

Exercise 9.5

For the past 6 years, a child has been attending the city's magnet school, which draws mostly upper-middle-class children. Because the school only teaches kindergarten and grades 1 through 5, the parents have to decide where to send the child next year. The parents agree that they want what is best for their child, but they have strong disagreements about what is best. One wants to send the child to an expensive private school arguing that the "best" children are going to that school. The other maintains that the "best" experience for a child is in public school. Neither one will concede. The child will have friends from the current school in both places and really does not seem to care about the decision. Suppose that one of the parents is your best friend seeking your advice. What would you say? Now suppose that the other one is your friend and asked for your advice instead. What would you say?

Analyzing Nonverbal Messages

Accurate perception of nonverbal messages helps to prevent and overcome impasses. In trying to understand what the other side wants, what it is willing to accept, what it is trying to say, and what it is trying to hide, negotiators rely on nonverbal analysis as a supplement to their listening skills (Hickson & Stacks, 1989). Many of the messages exchanged during negotiations are nonverbal, and the ability to make an accurate analysis adds to overall negotiating ability (Casse & Deol, 1985).

Anyone who has observed the early stages of a teenage romance knows the importance of nonverbal messages in human interaction. The strong desire to communicate is countered by a strong fear that a verbal message expressing interest might be immediately rejected. A nonverbal message can be sent with greater comfort because it offers the sender an escape route. Because nonverbal expression has no grammar to arbitrate meaning, a message can be sent, and, if it looks as if the answer is negative, the sender can gracefully back away. Young lovers and negotiators are able to transmit nonverbal messages without incurring such risks as losing face or making a premature commitment (Smith, 1988).

Nonverbal messages function in negotiation in much the same way as they function in the early stages of romance. Common messages are these: "We are now willing to talk." "We may be able to move a little more." "We think we can agree." Verbal messages make commitments. Nonverbal signals are important negotiation tools because they avoid commitment (Smith, 1988).

When negotiators carefully observe nonverbal behavior and try to analyze it, what do they want to know? What do they look for? Individual nonverbal signs may not have much communication value, but the other side's broad patterns of nonverbal behavior should be analyzed for general characteristics, state of mind, signs of how they think, react, and what seems to motivate them (Smith, 1988). Careful observation may yield indications that the message senders are nervous, frustrated, bored, angry, or unsure.

Another reason to examine nonverbal behavior is that observing and understanding the behaviors of others offer a sense of comfort and confidence. Personal power is conveyed primarily by nonverbal channels and understood by identifying nonverbal clues. Skilled analysts gain confidence from their ability to understand and block intimidation tactics (Illich, 1980).

A third use of nonverbal analysis is to scan for opportunities to enhance one's position or weaken the other side's power. Backing away from a strong stand, extending an offer, and deciding to be cooperative are all potentially risky communications, and, as such, they are often tentatively proposed by a nonverbal sign at first (Smith, 1988). If one side misses the other's sign, they may miss a favorable offer and perhaps even a chance at agreement.

Once the importance of nonverbal messages is realized, the next step is to recognize and interpret them. Invasions of personal space, attacks upon territory, and clues about agreement and confrontation are messages that signal the intentions of others. By looking at some of the major human warning systems, it is possible to make some systematic observations about nonverbal behavior.

The sense of personal space influences people's behavior regardless of whether or not they are conscious of it. Some people (and many similarities are culturally determined) stand close to others in conversations. Others are more comfortable at a relative distance. Negotiators will find that the habits of others give clues about their intentions. Do they move physically closer to emphasize the importance of their point? Do they crowd, point a finger, or touch when they talk? Do they ease back in the chair as a sign of encouragement for a response to their proposals? Do their gestures seem to be an exercise of power or superiority? Watching how people use space—that is, observing if they invade the space of others or if they respect it—provides clues about their intentions and strategies. Signs of dramatic changes in this behavior can be helpful for spotting potential substantial changes in attitudes and behaviors.

When someone moves close to another person as an attempt to intimidate her, it is seldom a good tactic for the recipient of this gesture to back away. As an alternative, she may want to stand her ground unfazed, or she may want to ridicule the other person's behavior, but backing away may signal fear or lack of confidence. On the other hand, a negotiator should not be seduced by someone's easy relaxed attitude that evokes a comfortable and conversational climate. Those who feel that they are talking too much or too freely should ask themselves if the other side is manipulating the dialogue.

Another method of using nonverbal behavior to make a statement is in the manipulation of territory. People structure their territory to make others comfortable or uneasy. Territory can be used to express power. The size of a desk or the luxuriousness of the furnishings may be used to make a point. Suggestions for changing the setting of negotiations may be a sign of attitude change on the other side. "Why don't we talk about this at the golf course?" indicates a different kind of attitude than "I see we are scheduled to meet back here at 2:00 tomorrow, try to be on time." A negotiator may be able to learn more about members of the other side by meeting in their territory or may feel more in control by meeting in his or her own. A neutral site is ideal for negotiations because it can be agreeable and comfortable for both sides and advantageous to neither. The general guideline for handling messages from the "territory" is that negotiators should not allow the setting to intimidate or seduce them. One who must negotiate on the other side's turf should not be awed by the environment. Negotiators who keep their goals in mind will find it possible to respect the other side's property without being awed by it. Negotiators should create and make small decisions totally on their own if they want to gain a feeling of control. Choosing where to sit (even if it means moving a chair), or even whether to sit, may help make a negotiator feel more confident. A negotiator should not let the other side treat her as if she were part of the furniture, but she will not want to feel so comfortable that she is lulled into an undesirable agreement. Thinking about territory and considering the impact of each negotiating setting can help a negotiator overcome the use of territory by the other side.

Another use of nonverbal behavior is to give clues about agreement and/or confrontation. The manipulation of the seating arrangement is one way that a negotiator can give or receive this type of clue. Negotiators often vie for a "power" position such as head of the table, center of a large delegation, back against a wall, and so on.

Those attempting to exercise power will often seek a place that ensures the attention of everyone in the room. Some negotiators gravitate toward the most prominent seat, but those who want to avoid a show of power will want to have an alternative plan. From the many studies examining seating arrangements or the shape of the negotiating table, the main issue is this: Does the configuration add to the adversarial urge or does it help dissipate the confrontation? The questions that negotiators should be asking about seating are these: Will it be advantageous? Will it make negotiations more of a direct confrontation? Will it ease tension and make an atmosphere more conducive for discussion? When the other side structures a face-to-face confrontation, are they stressing the importance of their message? Are they trying to intimidate? Are they simply expressing their will to prevail? Chances are that they may be acting out of custom or tradition, without any conscious effort to send a message. A skilled negotiator will deemphasize any single act and focus greater attention on the other side's patterns of behavior.

Success does not necessarily come to those who occupy the "power chairs." When the performance of teams sitting opposite each other was compared with that of teams who sat around a table alternating members from both sides, strong teams had more success when they were in the alternating seating arrangement (Stephenson & Kniveton, 1978). One explanation is that those who are perceived to have strong personal power may be met with resistance if they demonstrate additional power with nonverbal clues, while they gain greater acceptance when they attempt to diffuse resistance by sending signals to show that they are "just part of the gang."

Negotiators generally should strive to keep the sides balanced. If the other side wants to structure a face-to-face confrontation, a confident negotiator will not avoid it or appear intimidated. The skilled negotiator will watch, listen, and show an interest in the other side's proposals without giving away any unintentional messages. Those with control over the arrangement of the room will usually want to minimize the amount of direct confrontation to keep the other side talking as much as possible. Those who make members of the other side feel comfortable, free, and somewhat trusting have gained command over the environment.

Nonverbal signals may help to locate the barriers to agreement. Some disagreements are not over the issues. A personal problem or political difference may separate the negotiators and reduce the likelihood of agreement. Responses that form a pattern of unusually personal, passionate, hostile, or cold messages may indicate that it is necessary and appropriate for the negotiators to address the people problem before they try to resolve the issues.

Signs of acceptance and rejection are often sent nonverbally. The other side signals the negotiator, "OK, you have made your point, we agree (or, we give up)." Or they look as if they are saying, "Never! We do not care what you do or say, we do not agree." When negotiators receive either of these signals, they may have gone as far as possible. By continuing to talk, negotiators only give away their case and drain their bargaining power. They should halt the talks until another time or at least move to another issue.

By careful observation of nonverbal behavior, one can gain information, increase confidence, and pick up helpful cues about movement. Negotiators also can learn a lot about how they are seen by the other side. Those who wish to increase their control over their nonverbal messages may want to practice and observe their gestures and other nonverbal responses. Others will be more comfortable simply trying to build consistency between their words and their bodies.

Those who want to make an important point should know how much voice and mannerism can help convey the importance. By pausing for a second before introducing a major point, by speaking a little more slowly and a little more loudly, and certainly by using their faces and bodies to say, "this is important," negotiators can emphasize selected items. Deemphasis can also be managed nonverbally. If negotiators want to cool down a particularly hostile exchange, they can reduce the tension of their words, but they will also want to ease back with their bodies, lower their volume, and soften their facial expressions. Negotiators can increase effectiveness simply by learning how to present their nonverbal message in a manner consistent with their verbal message.

Negotiators who are skilled at observing and using nonverbal information are more likely to be more comfortable than those who have difficulty reading people. By understanding how nonverbal messages function and knowing what they can expect to learn, negotiators are more likely to find greater meaning. Finally, negotiators adept at monitoring for cues from spatial arrangement, territory, confrontational posture, and barriers should be able to improve their judgments about credibility and movement of the other side.

EXERCISE GUIDE

The moral of the story of Joni Jones and her parents at the beginning of the chapter: Joni and her parents cannot resolve the issue without making some change. If Joni tries to exert pressure, she may need some outside help. Perhaps her brothers would be willing to intervene, or maybe someone from the university can help persuade the parents that Joni should be able to continue her last year at the main campus. Ideally, someone from the parents' world would make the most credible ally for Joni. If she can find some source of financial support other than her parents, she can demonstrate that their power is not as awesome as it seems now. Finally, Joni can change the focus of the discussion and show her parents that they are responsible for financing her education if not her life-style. She may offer some concession to their life-style, perhaps agreeing to modify her living arrangements or behavior for the next year in exchange for support through graduation. Whatever her choices, she should show respect to her parents and their way of life while she changes the focus of the discussion toward the shared goal of her graduating.

EXERCISE 9.1 The discussion should focus the apparent causes of the impasse and attempt to fit the causes into one of the three categories: political or personal inflexibilities, misunderstanding or badly phrased proposals, or unreasonable expectations.

EXERCISE 9.2 When the other side is confused or unsure, you may want to exhibit strength and confidence in your position. Under these circumstances, a concession may be viewed as a sign of weakness or uncertainty.

EXERCISE 9.3 Under these circumstances, a small concession might produce some movement from the other side. If both sides have fairly complete information, the other side would be in a good position to know that the concession was genuine.

EXERCISE 9.4 Probably the best choice here would be to avoid or defuse the personal power of the other side and have the confrontation only on the issue.

EXERCISE 9.5 The advice to both parents should probably be the same. They should search for their areas of agreement about the child's welfare and try to uncover the child's "real" feelings about the preferred choice. The child's teachers might be a good source of objective information. The parents should make some ground rules. For example, once the decision is made, both will support it completely. They also may agree about the method they will use to make a selection. Once they have established some areas of broad agreement, the final joint decision may be easier to reach.

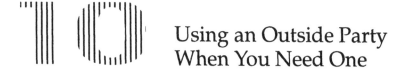 Using an Outside Party
When You Need One

The Case of the Divorce Settlement

Cindy and Doug have been divorced officially for 6 months. The proceedings were bitter. Doug developed a relationship with a younger woman about 2½ years ago. Cindy found out about the affair 2 years ago. For the next 6 months, the two of them alternately fought and reconciled, and then Doug walked out for good. In other circumstances, the two of them might have been able to walk away from the experience, try and forget the marriage, and move on to a new phase of life. But they have two children, ages 3 and 5.

Cindy tried to get as many of the assets as she could for herself and the kids, and Doug did not resist much. She was given possession and equity in the house, the new car, and a substantial amount of child support to be paid in equal monthly installments for the next 15 years. The deal was that Doug provide the fixed financial support and Cindy would determine how to spend it to provide for the welfare of the children.

Cindy is still very bitter. She feels that she was entitled to this generous settlement because Doug had left her, because Doug had hurt her, and because Doug's job paid twice as much as hers. Doug is resentful because he feels that Cindy would never agree to deal with their problems a few years before when he wanted to address them. He feels bitter because she "tried to take him for everything he had." He is prepared to live up to the terms of the settlement decided by the court but will not entertain any flexibility.

New circumstances have added to Cindy's general bitterness. It looks as if she will lose her job within the next 6 months and there are no comparable jobs in the area. She needs a year to complete her master's degree. She thinks that the economy might pick up a bit in that year and that the degree should offer her better prospects as well. Among the other circumstances, within a month after the settlement, Doug more than doubled his salary. Two weeks later, he won $1.2 million in the state lottery. He is very generous with the kids, buying them clothes and treating them to all sorts of entertainment, but he thinks that Cindy is obligated to maintain their standard of living with the agreed-on allowance.

Early U.S. colonists encouraged a negotiation tradition in the new land when they limited the role of government in favor of voluntary agreements between private parties. Their legacy is a tradition of negotiation as a private process occurring between the principal parties or their authorized agents. Outsiders are not usually welcomed in this process. This method works well in many cases. Negotiators of all kinds are usually able to identify common interests and reach agreement with others. Society generally benefits from these private agreements, because the need for regulatory power and administration is reduced and because the parties can more efficiently control their destinies. The process breaks down and creates suffering when one party has monopoly power, when the two parties conspire to injure or isolate another party, or when the two parties cannot reach agreement. In certain circumstances, government seeks to regulate monopoly power or provide access to groups who have been denied opportunities to enter the process.

Historically, failure to reach agreement has been viewed as a private decision or an unfortunate anomaly, but growing cities, a rising population, and developing technology have all made the world more interdependent. Now, when private parties fail to reach agreement, the result may be costly for many others who have no voice in the process. If labor and management fail to reach agreements, the lockouts or strikes may have far-reaching effects that inconvenience parties outside the dispute. When cities and major league franchise owners fail to agree on the size, shape, or terms of a municipal facility and the team moves away, many residents feel an economic loss. As a result of the growing interdependence, several governmental and private agencies have acquired the mission of assisting private parties to resolve their disputes. The major types of roles that these outside parties play in dispute resolutions include the following:

1. Fact-finding is a process in which someone outside the dispute examines the facts surrounding the case and makes a recommendation to both parties. The power to discover and recommend is usually the only tool available to the fact finder.

2. Mediation and conciliation are processes that require both sides to agree on an outside party to help them continue the negotiating process and move beyond the issues causing impasse by making suggestions and clarifying the problems. Some mediators hold a more aggressive view of their role. They see themselves as taking charge of the negotiations and pressuring the sides into agreement. Kolb (1983a, 1983b) found some evidence that more aggressive mediators did produce fast settlements in many cases but those mediators who applied less pressure were more likely to promote an eventual settlement. In neither of the cases do mediators have the power to decide for the parties.

3. Arbitration is a process in which the negotiators on both sides recognize that they will not be able to reach a voluntary agreement. Both sides agree to select an outsider who will hear each side's case and make a decision, and both parties agree to abide by the decision. Final-offer arbitration is a special kind of arbitration in which the arbitrator only hears the final offer from each side and chooses one or the other. This special procedure was designed to force each side into making their most reasonable proposal in the hope that they would overcome the impasse on their own.

4. Litigation is a process where one of the parties alleges that the other has violated his legal rights. The aggrieved party brings a lawsuit against the other, attempting to prevent an undesired behavior or to seek payment for damages.

When is third-party intervention necessary? Three major signs suggest that outside help may be advantageous to a negotiator:

1. when both parties realize that they will not be able to reach agreement on their own,
2. when one of the parties sees their own demands as reasonable and the other side as unreasonable and unlikely to move, and
3. in special circumstances with unusual problems such as technical issues, legal issues, or disputes involving several parties.

Exercise 10.1

There is a row of pines that grow on the borderline between your house and your neighbor's house. You always liked the trees because they blocked the cold north wind in the winter and gave you a sense of privacy. Today, your neighbor had his chain saw fired up and was ready to cut down the whole row. He said the trees block the winter sun and increase his heating bills. He stopped when you asked him to stop, but the incident is not over. You have always had a friendly but not close relationship and want to maintain it. You want the trees to stay. He wants them down. The only thing you agree on is that the trees are exactly on the borderline. What can you do? Do you need someone to help you with your dispute?

McCarthy and Shorett (1984) provide an example of a structure that requires an outside party:

Environmental disputes may involve as many as 15 or 20 separate interest groups, each maintaining distinct viewpoints on the issues in dispute. The large number of parties fundamentally alters the dynamics of the negotiations. Negotiations must be structured to accommodate an elongated time frame so that the negotiators can report back to their constituencies, discuss negotiating possibilities, and receive their constituencies' endorsement for new positions. Time is also needed for small group meetings to consider and resolve issues that may be important to only a few representatives. Multiparty representation often requires mediation between groups that hold basically similar positions. In many instances, the mediator will devote as much if not more attention to disagreements between environmental groups than to the fundamental differences between these groups and business or other interests that espouse sharply contrasting positions. (p. 2)

The principal parties often feel fear, contempt, or suspicion toward external intervention. Even in deeply troubled marriages, one or both spouses often resist counseling. Outside neutrals have a role to play in the negotiation process, but negotiators worry that outsiders may overwhelm the parties or will effect a result no better than one the parties could have reached independently. Negotiation scholars worry that having procedures allowing easy access to third-party intervention encourages the principals to abdicate their negotiating role and become too heavily reliant upon arbitrators (Extejt & Chelius, 1985). Those who are pressured to reach agreement, because they see no hope or have no mechanism to reach a third party, are more likely to negotiate seriously.

Exercise 10.2

You work in an office that offers support services for adults returning to college. The atmosphere in your workplace had been casual and comfortable until 2 years ago, when a new person was hired. He has initiated several new and valuable programs but has alienated you and your coworkers with his aggressive style, his unsolicited advice, and his competitiveness. He brags about how often he has to "bail out" his coworkers. Any attempts to talk with him end with a vigorous denial and a claim that everyone else is jealous of his talent and work. Your boss avoids confronting problems by minimizing them, saying that everything will settle down if you just allow a little time. Do you think you can settle the problems on your own? Do you need someone to come in and help make some changes? What kind of person do you need? How would your boss and coworkers react to an outside "helper"?

Effects of Third-Party Intervention on the Negotiation Process

Most labor agreements prescribe binding arbitration as the remedy for grievances that reach an impasse. A few agreements include provisions for arbitration should contract negotiations break down. The theory is that production will continue without disruption and the arbitrator will settle any disagreements. In labor relations, the existence of strike procedures and the threat of strikes result in the expenditure of greater time bargaining than under conditions that offer arbitration procedures and the likelihood of arbitration (Champlin & Bognanno, 1985). Magenau (1983) also found that negotiators are more likely to reach agreement on their own under strike conditions than under a forced arbitration procedure. Strikes and the threat of strikes may promote more earnest negotiation, but, because they are potentially disruptive to the parties and also to the outside world, there is pressure to eliminate them. Extejt and Chelius (1985) found that impasse procedures deter but do not eliminate strikes. Strikes that occur when arbitration is available are often associated with lengthy delays in implementing the impasse procedure. The trade-off appears to be between better agreements with a possibility of strikes under strike procedures and inferior agreements but with less risk of strikes under alternate impasse procedures with third-party neutrals. In addition to affecting the agreement and the procedure, intervention has an effect on the principal parties. Johnson and Tullar (1972) found that those who require face-saving tend to respond negatively to the likelihood of third-party intervention. They also have greater distance between their first offer and their final settlement.

Exercise 10.3

A resident of a senior citizen's apartment complex celebrated her 95th birthday with the realization that it was not possible for her to live alone any longer. The person's two children argue constantly about what to do. One favors a nursing home and the other favors inviting the parent to each home for 6-month alternating periods and hiring someone to help with the care. The children have investigated all the local nursing homes together and analyzed the costs and problems likely to occur with an aged parent in the home. They have to make a decision now, but neither side will budge. Both love their mother and claim that their own position is the best for her. What problems would they have in selecting and using a third party?

Which Type of Third-Party
Intervention Works Best?

Mature formal agreements usually include dispute resolution
procedures to use when the parties fail to reach agreement on their
own. A mediator or fact-finder is often used as a first preference
and arbitrators or courts as a last resort. Traditionally, mediators
have been perceived as conciliators, and arbitrators as threateners.
Conciliation techniques seem to work best in short-term situations, when negotiations are primarily interpersonal and when
negotiators are agents not closely tied to the party or the issue. In
long-term, structured negotiations with ego-involved personalities, negotiators seem more suspicious of outside involvement.
Arbitration produces better results in pressuring parties to negotiate with each other when it is seldom used (Webb, 1986).

McCarthy and Shorett (1984) found that mediation is cheaper
than litigation. They also found that

> the emphasis on cost overshadows an equally important aspect
> relating to the quality of the decisions. In contrast to judicial review,
> which typically examines whether the administrative and proce-
> dural requirements have been adequately addressed, a mediated
> settlement deals directly with the substance of the dispute. It is this
> crucial aspect of the mediation process that should over the long run,
> encourage greater use of the process. (p. 2)

Still, arbitration and litigation offer other advantages. Johnson
and Pruitt (1972) found that negotiators faced with a binding
decision from a third party are more conciliatory in negotiations
and are more likely to reach agreement than those facing a non-
binding decision.

If negotiations with mediation cannot bring an agreement, arbitration may be necessary. Of the several types of arbitration, the
prospect of final-offer arbitration probably produces more serious
attempts to reach agreement by the parties than other types.
Magenau (1983) concludes: Negotiators facing the prospect of
final-offer arbitration are more likely to narrow the distance between the sides than those facing conventional arbitration prospects. Other major studies support this finding. Subbarao (1978)

found that final-offer arbitration pressures parties toward genuine negotiation, while last-offer-by-issue systems tend to undercut the bargaining process (Erickson, Holmes, Frey, Walker, & Thibut, 1974). Final-offer arbitration has strong effects on the individual negotiators. Faced with the prospect of final-offer arbitration, risk takers become even more competitive and demanding (Barr, 1987), but those who anticipate final-offer arbitration have lower aspirations and greater likelihood of reaching a settlement on their own than those who anticipate conventional arbitration (Starke & Notz, 1981).

Third-party intervention is not always desirable. The preferred path is for parties to reach an agreement on their own. If they fail to agree, however, outside parties provide a necessary and valuable service. Should one party request outside intervention, that outsider should be acceptable to the other side. A prearranged procedure for selection helps to minimize the risks of additional conflict, but, when parties have not made prior provisions, the outsider should truly be outside the process, disinterested, professional, and unconnected to either party. When one side wants an outsider to help resolve the dispute, it is nearly always a mistake for that side to push for the intervention of a specific person. A fair process and a lasting agreement require a neutral third party who works for both sides.

Exercise 10.4

John and Mary found out yesterday that they have inherited $50,000. What should have been a pleasant day ended in the worst argument they have had. Mary insists that the money should go into certificates of deposit. John is just as adamant that they spend at least half of the money on a few items that they had always fantasized about. Mary wants the two of them to talk with her father, who is a knowledgeable investment banker. What would you say if you were John? How would you respond if you were Mary? As a disinterested outsider, what advice would you give the couple?

EXERCISE GUIDE

The moral of the divorce settlement story at the beginning of the chapter: Cindy and Doug do not appear to be ready to renegotiate the terms of their divorce. Doug hurt Cindy and Cindy retaliated. Now Doug feels resentful and vindicated. Cindy feels resentful and aggrieved. Cindy will not be likely to get Doug to change the agreement to help her in any way. Cindy will not have much luck trying to make Doug feel guilty. He lives up to the written agreement and even does more for his kids. It appears that Cindy is the one who has failed the agreement. She is losing her job and has changed her mind about what she wants from him. The atmosphere does not seem likely to allow a new agreement at this time.

If Cindy wants to renegotiate, she needs to create a better climate for discussion. Even if she succeeds in reopening the talks, she has little chance of prodding Doug into granting her new favorable terms. Probably her best hope is to show Doug a plan that will benefit his two children without giving Cindy anything.

EXERCISE 10.1 It seems clear that there are not many options. Two neighbors who want to stay on good terms with each other do not have much room to accomplish their personal goals and still accommodate the needs of the other. In this case, the issue needs to be resolved, but the two parties might need help.

EXERCISE 10.2 If one employee is disrupting an organization, it is management's responsibility to correct the situation, but sometimes a supervisor is afraid to confront an employee. If peer pressure from fellow employees fails to change the worker's behavior, someone may have to intervene. Usually a higher level manager may receive a complaint stemming from a fellow employee, but those complaints usually do not address the real conflicts. An outside consultant could be called upon, but the rationale would be suspect and the affected parties probably would be suspicious if not hostile. The supervisor is the preferred choice, but, if he or she is unresponsive, the employees may have to deal with their coworker informally and directly.

EXERCISE 10.3 Individuals with family problems resist going to the outside for help because of a sense of self-reliance, privacy, or even shame. This situation may call for outside help, either a health care professional or a family counselor. Because both children feel concern and want to provide loving and appropriate care, a personal confrontation could leave lasting bitterness. The professional can provide an objective and expert assessment of the situation and perhaps offer some options that the parties could not have identified on their own.

EXERCISE 10.4 The two of them should talk with a financial adviser, but probably not Mary's father.

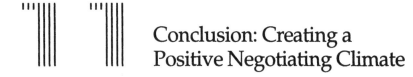

Conclusion: Creating a
Positive Negotiating Climate

The negotiation climate has a profound impact on the process and outcome of the negotiation. The physical and emotional environment creates comfort or anxiety, hostility or goodwill. Negotiation occurs in a place. People who bargain in their own physical environment can structure the space to a bargaining advantage. They have the option of making the other side feel as a welcomed guest who should be grateful for the invitation or as an intruder who is out of place and behaving illegitimately. Visual cues can give a clear demonstration of power. A well-appointed office, expensive clothing and jewelry, and a physical presentation of confidence all contribute to a picture of power. Negotiators will want to assess the physical environment of the bargaining. There are three major considerations:

- How can the physical environment be used to project comfort and confidence?
- Is it practical to negotiate at a site that offers a better setting to state and discuss proposals?
- If negotiators must meet in a setting that is intimidating, can they identify each of the factors that contribute to that discomfort and deal with each factor separately?

Relationships between bargainers may be warm, congenial, frosty, or hostile. Situations often predetermine emotional climate. Obviously, negotiators with unresolved grievances are likely to be angry. Less obvious are the structures that pressure or allow negotiators to be kind and gentle to each other and keep their anger hidden. People who work in the helping professions, such as social work, counseling, and teaching, often feel obliged to remain "professional" and avoid any image that appears to be selfish or aggressive. People in a long-term, highly valued relationship often have a hard time expressing anger or discontent with the relationship. As a consequence, hidden below the surface, there are often resentments that influence behavior even if they do not actually appear.

To a limited extent, it is possible for one side to exert control over the emotional climate by determining what the climate is likely to be. A negotiator will want to create a climate where the other side feels comfortable talking. Gibb (1961) identified some of the perceptions that make people defensive and closed. He contrasted each with a corresponding perception that builds a supportive emotional climate for communication.

Defensive	*Supportive*
Evaluation	Description
Strategy	Spontaneity
Control	Task Orientation
Superiority	Equality
Neutrality	Empathy
Certainty	Provisionalism

Gibb's analysis argues that those who give the impression that they are evaluating, using strategy and manipulation, concerned with bossing or control, acting superior, measuring people against standards or other reference points, and certain about all of their opinions and observations are very likely to make people feel defensive and make them reluctant to disclose themselves or their positions very much. On the other hand, those who make their audience feel comfortable are speakers who describe what they see or feel rather than evaluate, who appear to be spontaneous rather than strategic, who focus on the tasks rather than on control, who make the audience feel equal rather than inferior, who seek to understand the particular feeling and circumstance of the audience rather than generalizing a problem into something ordinary, and who qualify or allow for possible exceptions to their own conclusions.

Carnevale and Lawler (1986) examined the effects of time pressure and deadlines in negotiation and found that, in an uncooperative climate, time pressures produce increased competitiveness, stronger demands, and lower outcomes, but, in a cooperative climate, time pressures tend to bring about greater information exchange, greater willingness to lower demands, and mutual search for an agreement. In presenting a case, the emotional climate may depend not only on what is said but how it is said. There are times when someone may want to create a defensive climate in negotiations. Because, however, bargaining power comes from what is learned about the other side, negotiators will usually want to keep communication channels open and working.

The occasion contributes to the balance of power because it often defines the purpose of negotiations. Do the parties come together to maintain or expand a satisfactory relationship? Do they want to solve a mutual problem? Of the many reasons for negotiations, one useful perspective is to ask whether the other side wants permanence or change. Is their desire to extend or solidify the status quo? Do they like things as they are and fear change? Or does the accumulation of grievances make them want to seek radical change in the agreement?

In many cases, the occasion helps to identify the other side's motives. A large part of negotiators' power is generated as they learn the desires of their counterpart. Once a negotiator finds what the members of the other side value and what they consider to be less important, he or she will learn what is available for trade and how much compliance is worth to the other side. By recognizing what the other side seeks, negotiators are able to make their proposals within a framework of mutual pursuit of changes that will resolve differences.

Finally, the negotiators' intensity can dramatically affect the bargaining environment. Those with strong feelings about a few clear, simple goals have an added advantage. The advantage remains with the negotiators who can maintain their own intensity but not provoke equally strong passion on the other side. Terry Herndon (1976) accounted for the dramatic growth in public sector unions during the 1970s in the United States in terms of the militancy among public workers: "It's simple. Spurn a moderate and create a militant. The price of stability is equity. Deny equity and induce instability" (p. 12).

Negotiators may have the power to reject unreasonable or even reasonable demands. They may feel that they have the right or perhaps the obligation to dismiss them, but, before they do, they should try to anticipate the reaction of the other side. Will the action totally frustrate the other side's effort or will it create a greater resolve to fight back? Negotiators may have to confront intensity on the other side, but they should be careful not to create additional resistance or crystallize whatever resistance exists.

As they prepare for a specific encounter, negotiators should consider the physical climate, the emotional climate, the purpose of the negotiation for both parties, and the intensity with which both sides enter into the situation. By analyzing these aspects of the negotiation environment throughout the talks, they should be able to exercise some control over these factors and their effects.

References

Abboush, S. (1987). Union leaders' willingness to negotiate concessions. *Journal of Labor Research, 8*, 47-58.

Alward, J. M. (1984). Toward negotiations. *Public Personnel Management Journal, 13*(2), 191-196.

An Apology. (1991, January 3). *Wall Street Journal*, p. C22.

Atkinson, G. (1973). Bargaining rules of the game. *Personnel Management, 8*(2), 21-24.

Axelrod, R. (1984). *The evolution of cooperation*. New York: Basic Books.

Axthelm, P. (1982). Wasted days, wasted nights. *Newsweek, 100*, 113.

Bacharach, S. B., & Lawler, E. J. (1981). *Bargaining: Power, tactics, and outcomes*. San Francisco: Jossey-Bass.

Baldwin, D. A. (1976). Bargaining with airline hijackers. In E. Zartman (Ed.), *The 50 percent solution* (pp. 204-249). New York: Anchor.

Barr, S. H. (1987). Risk aversion and negotiator behavior in public sector arbitration. *Journal of Collective Negotiations in the Public Sector, 16*(2), 99-115.

Barrett, J. T. (1990). A win-win approach to collective bargaining: The PAST model. *Labor Law Journal, 41*(1), 41-44.

Bartos, O. J. (1977). Simple model of negotiation: A sociological point of view. *Journal of Conflict Resolution, 24*, 565-579.

Boulding, K. (1977). The power of nonconflict. *Journal of Social Issues, 33*, 28-29.

Bulkeley, W. M. (1985, March 25). Sports agents help athletes win and keep those super salaries. *Wall Street Journal*, p. 31.

Burton, L. (1987). *Ethical aspects of public sector negotiation: Concepts, cases, and commentary*. Washington, DC: National Institute for Dispute Resolution.

Byrnes, J. F. (1987). Ten guidelines for effective negotiating. *Business Horizons, 30*(3), 7-12.

Carnegie, D. (1952). *How to win friends and influence people*. New York: Simon & Schuster.

Carnevale, P. J., & Lawler, E. J. (1986). Time pressure and the development of integrative agreements in bilateral negotiations. *Journal of Conflict Resolution, 30*, 636-659.

Casse, P., & Deol, S. (1985). *Managing intercultural negotiations: Guidelines for trainers and negotiators*. Washington, DC: Sietar International.

Champlin, F. C., & Bognanno, M. F. (1985). Time spent processing interest arbitration cases: The Minnesota experience. *Journal of Collective Negotiations in the Public Sector, 14*, 53-65.

Chatterjee, K., & Lilien, G. L. (1984). Efficiency of alternative bargaining procedures. *Journal of Conflict Resolution, 28*, 270-295.

Daniels, V. (1967). Communication, incentive, and structural variables in interpersonal exchange and negotiation. *Journal of Experimental Social Psychology, 3*, 47-74.

DeNisi, A. S., & Dworkin, J. B. (1981). Final-offer arbitration and the naive negotiator. *Industrial and Labor Relations Review, 35*(1), 78-87.

Donohue, W. A. (1978). An empirical framework for examining negotiation processes and outcomes. *Speech Monographs, 45*, 247-257.

Druckman, D. (1986). Stages, turning points, and crises: Negotiating military base rights, Spain and the United States. *Journal of Conflict Resolution, 30*(2), 327-360.

Duane, M. J., Azevedo, R. E., & Anderson, U. (1985). Behavior as an indicator of an opponent's intentions in collective negotiations. *Psychological Reports, 57*, 507-513.

Dunlop, J. T. (1984). *Dispute resolution: Negotiation and consensus building.* Dover, MA: Auburn House.

DuToit, P. (1989). Bargaining about bargaining: Inducing the self-negating prediction in deeply divided societies—the case of South Africa. *Journal of Conflict Resolution, 33*(2), 210-230.

Dwyer, F. R. (1984). Are two better than one? Bargaining behavior and outcomes in asymmetrical power relationships. *Journal of Consumer Research, 11*, 680-690.

Erickson, B., Holmes, J. G., Frey, R., Walker, L., & Thibut, J. (1974). Functions of a third party in the resolution of conflict: The role of a judge in pretrial conferences. *Journal of Personality and Social Psychology, 30*, 293-306.

Extejt, M. M., & Chelius, J. R. (1985). The behavioral impact of impasse resolution procedures. *Review of Public Personnel Administration, 5*(2), 37-48.

Feinstein, J. (1986). *A season on the brink: A year with Bob Knight and the Indiana Hoosiers.* New York: Macmillan.

Fisher, R., & Brown, S. (1988). *Getting together: Building a relationship that gets to yes.* Boston: Houghton Mifflin.

Fisher, R., & Ury, W. (1981). *Getting to yes: Negotiating agreement without giving in.* New York: Penguin.

Friedman, T. L. (1984, October 7). The power of fanatics. *The New York Times Magazine*, pp. 32-35ff.

Galowitz, S. W. (1979). Selling the flawed property. *Real Estate Review, 9*, 25-30.

Gibb, J. R. (1961). Defensive communication. *Journal of Communication, 11*, 141-148.

Goleman, D. (1985). *Vital lies, simple truths: The psychology of self-deception.* New York: Simon & Schuster.

Gordon, J. (1990). Teaching kids to negotiate. *Newsweek, 115*, 65.

Gouray, R. (1987). Negotiations and bargaining. *Management Decision, 25*(3), 16-27.

Greenhalgh, L., Neslin, S. A., & Gilkey, R. W. (1985). The effects of negotiator preferences, situational power, and negotiator personality on outcomes of business negotiations. *Academy of Management Journal, 28*(1), 9-33.

Hamner, W. C., & Harnett, D. L. (1975). The effects of information and aspiration level on bargaining behavior. *Journal of Experimental Social Psychology, 11*, 329-342.

Hermann, M. G., & Kogan, N. (1968). Negotiations in leader and delegate groups. *Journal of Conflict Resolution, 12*, 332-344.

Hermone, R. H. (1974). How to negotiate . . . and come out the winner. *Management Review, 63*(11), 19-25.

Herndon, T. (1976). Public workers and the New South: Collective bargaining and the public sector. *Vital Speeches, 43*, 10-13.

Hickson, M. I., III, & Stacks, D. W. (1989). *Nonverbal communication: Studies and applications.* Dubuque, IA: William C Brown.

Hill, R. (1979). The subtle art of negotiation. *International Management, 34*(9), 28-30.

Huber, V., & Neale, M. A. (1986). Effects of cognitive heuristics and goals on negotiator performance and subsequent goal setting. *Organizational Behavior and Human Decision Processes, 38,* 342-365.

Illich, J. (1980). *The art and skill of successful negotiation.* Englewood Cliffs, NJ: Prentice-Hall.

Jandt, F. E., & Gillette, P. (1985). *Win-win negotiating: Turning conflict into agreement.* New York: John Wiley.

Jennings, K. M., Paulson, S. K., & Williamson, S. A. (1987). Fact-finding in perspective. *Government Union Review, 8*(3), 54-70.

Johnson, D. F., & Pruitt, D. G. (1972). Preintervention effects of mediation versus arbitration. *Journal of Applied Psychology, 56,* 1-10.

Johnson, D. F., & Tullar, W. L. (1972). Style of third party intervention, face-saving and bargaining behavior. *Journal of Experimental Social Psychology, 8,* 319-330.

Johnson, D. W. (1971). Effects of warmth of interaction, accuracy of understanding, and the proposal of compromise on listener's behavior. *Journal of Counseling Psychology, 18*(3), 207-216.

Johnson, R. A. (1985). Grievance negotiation: An analysis of factors popularly associated with success. *Labor Studies Journal, 9*(3), 271-278.

Jones, S. G. (1989). Have your lawyer call my lawyer: Bilateral delegation in bargaining situations. *Journal of Economic Behavior and Organization, 11,* 159-174.

Kasprzak, J. F. (1986). The side bar: A last stab at accord. *Personnel, 63*(2), 10-13.

Klimoski, R. J. (1972). The effects of intragroup forces on intergroup conflict resolution. *Organizational Behavior and Human Performance, 8,* 363-383.

Klimoski, R. J., & Breaugh, J. A. (1977). When performance doesn't count: A constituency looks at its spokesman. *Organizational Behavior and Human Performance, 20,* 301-311.

Kolb, D. M. (1983a). *The mediators.* Cambridge: MIT Press.

Kolb, D. M. (1983b). Strategy and the tactics of mediation. *Human Relations, 36*(3), 247-268.

Komorita, S. S. (1977). Negotiating from strength and the concept of bargaining strength. *Journal for the Theory of Social Behavior, 7,* 65-79.

Lamm, H., & Kogan, N. (1970). Risk-taking in the context of intergroup negotiations. *Journal of Experimental Social Psychology, 6,* 351-363.

Lasch, C. (1978). *The culture of narcissism: American life in an age of diminishing expectations.* New York: Norton.

Lawler, E. J. (1975). The impact of status differences on coalitional agreements. *Journal of Conflict Resolution, 19,* 271-285.

Lax, D. A., & Sebenius, J. K. (1985). The power of alternatives or the limits to negotiation. *Negotiation Journal, 1,* 163-180.

Leap, T. L., & Oliva, T. A. (1981). Public sector multilateral collective bargaining: A microeconomic analysis. *Journal of Collective Negotiations in the Public Sector, 10*(4), 287-307.

Magenau, J. M. (1983). The impact of alternative impasse procedures on bargaining: A laboratory experiment. *Industrial and Labor Relations Review, 36,* 361-377.

Mankin, L. D. (1977). Public employee organizations: The quest for legitimacy. *Public Personnel Management, 6,* 334-340.

McCarthy, J., & Shorett, A. (1984). *Negotiating settlements: A guide to environmental mediation.* New York: American Arbitration Association.

McCarthy, W. (1985). The role of power and principle in getting to yes. *Negotiation Journal, 1,* 59-66.

McCroskey, J. C., & Young, T. J. (1981). Ethos and credibility: The construct and its measurement after three decades. *Central States Speech Journal, 32*(2), 24-36.

Michner, H. A., Vaske, J. J., Schleifer, S. I., Plazewski, J. G., & Chapman, L. J. (1975). Factors affecting concession rate and the threat usage in bilateral conflict. *Sociometry, 38,* 62-80.

Miller, A. (1949). *Death of a salesman.* New York: Viking.

Molloy, J. T. (1975). *Dress for success.* New York: Warner.

Morley, I. E., & Stephenson, G. M. (1970). Formality in experimental negotiations: A validation study. *Journal of Psychology, 61,* 383-384.

Neale, M. A., & Bazerman, M. H. (1985a). Perspectives for understanding negotiation: Viewing negotiation as a judgmental process. *Journal of Conflict Resolution, 29,* 33-55.

Neale, M. A., & Bazerman, M. H. (1985b). The effects of framing and negotiator overconfidence on bargaining behaviors and outcomes. *Academy of Management Journal, 28,* 34-49.

Nierenberg, G. I. (1971). *Creative business negotiating: Skills and successful strategies.* New York: Hawthorn.

Peale, N. V. (1952). *The power of positive thinking.* Englewood Cliffs, NJ: Prentice-Hall.

Pruitt, D. G., & Drews, J. L. (1969). The effect of time pressure, time elapsed, and the opponent's concession rate on behavior in negotiation. *Journal of Experimental Social Psychology, 5,* 43-60.

Pruitt, D. G., & Lewis, S. A. (1975). Development of integrative solutions in bilateral negotiation. *Journal of Personality and Social Psychology, 31,* 621-633.

Reban, H. (1977). Building a counterforce to multinational corporations. *Monthly Labor Review, 100,* 46-47.

Reisman, B., & Compa, L. (1985). The case for adversarial unions. *Harvard Business Review, 63*(3), 22-36.

Ringer, R. J. (1973). *Winning through intimidation.* New York: Fawcett Crest.

Rozzelle, R. M. (1971). Role playing vs. laboratory deception: A comparison of methods in the study of compromising behavior. *Psychonomic Science, 25*(4), 241-243.

Rubin, J. Z., & DiMatteo, M. R. (1972). Factors affecting the magnitude of subjective utility parameters in a tacit bargaining game. *Journal of Experimental Social Psychology, 8,* 412-426.

Saunders, H. H. (1985). We need a larger theory of negotiation: The importance of pre-negotiating phases. *Negotiation Journal 1,* 249-262.

Schulz, J. W., & Pruitt, D. G. (1978). The effects of mutual concern on joint welfare. *Journal of Experimental Social Psychology, 14,* 480-492.

Schurr, P. H., & Ozanne, J. L. (1985). Influences on exchange processes: Buyers' preconceptions of a seller's trustworthiness and bargaining toughness. *Journal of Consumer Research, 11,* 939-953.

Short, J. A. (1974). Effects of communication on experimental negotiation. *Human Relations, 27,* 225-234.

Smith, D. H. (1969). Communication and negotiation outcome. *The Journal of Communication, 19,* 248-256.

Smith, H. B. (1988). *Selling through negotiation: The handbook of sales negotiation.* New York: American Management Association.

Sondak, H., & Bazerman, M. H. (1989). Matching and negotiation processes in quasi-markets. *Organizational Behavior and Human Decision Processes, 44,* 261-280.

Spector, B. I. (1977). Negotiation as a psychological process. *Journal of Conflict Resolution, 24,* 607-618.

Spiro, R. L., & Perreault, W. D. (1979). Influence use by industrial salesmen: Influence-strategy mixes and situational determinants. *Journal of Business, 52,* 435-455.

Starke, F. A., & Notz, W. W. (1981). Pre- and post-intervention effects of conventional versus final offer arbitration. *Academy of Management Journal, 24,* 832-850.

Stensrud, R. (1985). Type A behavior pattern and tendency to cooperate or compete during a simulated negotiation activity. *Psychological Reports, 57,* 917-918.

Stephenson, G. M., & Brotherton, J. (1975). Social progression and polarization: A study of discussion and negotiation in groups of mining supervisors. *British Journal of Social Clinical Psychology, 14,* 241-252.

Stephenson, G. M., & Kniveton, B. K. (1978). Interpersonal and interparty exchange: An experimental study of the effect of seating position on the outcome of negotiations between teams representing parties in dispute. *Human Relations, 31,* 555-566.

Streufert, S., Streufert, S. C., & Castore, C. H. (1968). Leadership in negotiations and the complexity of conceptual structure. *Journal of Applied Psychology, 52,* 218-223.

Subbarao, A. V. (1978). The impact of binding interest arbitration on negotiation and process outcome. *Journal of Conflict Resolution, 22,* 79-103.

Tedeschi, J. T., Schlenker, B. R., & Bonoma, T. V. (1975). Compliance to threats as a function of source attractiveness and esteem. *Sociometry, 38,* 81-98.

Terry, M. (1977). The inevitable growth of informality. *British Journal of Industrial Relations, 15,* 76-90.

Thompson, L. L., Mannix, E. A., & Bazerman, M. H. (1988). Group negotiations: Effects of the decision rule, agenda, and aspiration. *Journal of Personality and Social Psychology, 54,* 86-95.

Tjosvold, D. (1977). The effects of the constituent's affirmation and the opposing negotiator's self-presentation in bargaining between unequal status groups. *Organizational Behavior and Human Performance, 18,* 146-157.

Tjosvold, D., & Huston, T. L. (1978). Social-face and resistance to compromise in bargaining. *Journal of Social Psychology, 104,* 57-68.

Ury, W. L., Brett, J. M., & Goldberg, S. B. (1988). *Getting disputes resolved: Designing systems to cut conflict.* San Francisco: Jossey-Bass.

Wall, J. A. (1977). Operantly conditioning and negotiator's concession making. *Journal of Experimental Social Psychology, 13,* 431-440.

Wall, J. A. (1985). *Negotiation: Theory and practice.* Glenview, IL: Scott, Foresman.

Ways, M. (1979). The virtues, dangers, and limits of negotiation. *Fortune, 99,* 86-90.

Webb, J. (1986). Third parties at work: Conflict resolution or social control? *Journal of Occupational Psychology, 59,* 247-258.

Weiss-Wik, S. (1983). Enhancing negotiators' successfulness: Self-help books and related empirical research. *Journal of Conflict Resolution, 27*(4), 706-739.

Wills, G. (1982). The Kennedy imprisonment: The prisoner of toughness. *The Atlantic Monthly, 249*(2), 52-66.

Yukl, G. A. (1974). Effects of situational variables and opponent concessions on a bargainer's perception, aspiration, and concessions. *Journal of Personality and Social Psychology, 29,* 227-236.

Zartman, I. W. (1985). Negotiating from asymmetry: The North-South stalemate. *Negotiation Journal, 1,* 121-138.

Zemke, R. (1980). Negotiation skills training: Helping others get what they want—gracefully. *Training, 17*(2), 25-28.

Index

About the Author

Ralph A. Johnson, Professor in the School of Business at the University of Alabama at Birmingham, is Director of the Center for Labor Education and Research. He has studied labor relations and workplace conflict for two decades. He has written and lectured extensively about conflict resolution in private relationships and public issues. He received his Ph.D. and M.A. from Indiana University in Speech Communication and a B.A. in Communication Arts from Indiana University at South Bend.

Lightning Source UK Ltd.
Milton Keynes UK
UKHW040126150119
335593UK00001B/15/P